UNTYING THE YELLOW RIBBON

Transforming How Veterans and Communities Thrive

BY GRETCHEN MARTENS
Founder and CEO, Troops to Towns
Founder and CEO, Homeward Deployed

ISBN 978-0-9895102-0-2;

Inquiries: Info@VillageOfCare.com

Printed in the United States of America.

Ordering Information: Purchases of 1 to 100 at www.UntyingTheYellowRibbon.com and www.Amazon.com. Quantity soft-cover purchases and licenses for Kindle or Nook versions are available with special discounts for cities, counties, school systems, colleges and universities, nonprofits, and associations. Affiliate relationships can be established for fundraising by organizations with aligned missions to support Veterans or build community. Distribution by U.S. trade bookstores and wholesalers. For details, contact the publisher at the address above.

Book design by Dylan Halpern

This book is dedicated to my children, Caitlin and Dylan, who have patiently grown from teenagers into amazing young adults, sacrificing along with me as I struggled to establish Homeward Deployed and ease the transition period for America's post-9/11 Veterans, Guard, and Reserve. I hope that, at the end of the day, I make you proud and you feel like the ups and downs of life with me were worth it.

TABLE OF CONTENTS

PREFACE

Don't believe that the spirit of America is dead. After the planes hit the twin towers on September 11, 2001, nearly half a million people were trapped in lower Manhattan. Regular people organized hundreds of boats to evacuate them from the island in under nine hours....with no training, no money, and no time to plan. Just regular people stepping up to help, creating the largest boat lift evacuation in the history of the world....because other Americans needed them, and because they could. I challenge you to watch the You Tube documentary "Boatlift: An Untold Tale of 9/11 Resilience," narrated by Tom Hanks, and disagree.

But, we have forgotten how to BE community. We have forgotten how to roll up our sleeves, solve our own problems, and take care of our own people. The spirit of America that we saw re-emerge after 9/11 was smothered as we allowed ourselves to become divided as citizens over politics, taxes, immigration, religion, abortion, gay marriage, and now sequestration.

I've thought for more than a decade about how we heal the divide and come back to who we really are as a nation. And, in the course of the work I do with our military coming home, I think I've stumbled upon a solution. There is one issue that everyone agrees on, perhaps the only issue, and that is that no one in America wants to lose another generation of Veterans like we did after Vietnam.

I've talked to old people, young people....Democrats, Republicans... rich people, poor people....immigrants....pacifists....and everyone agrees. Everyone.

So, what do YOU think? Can this be one thing that we all agree on? Can we work together as we end our wars and bring our Veterans home....to make sure that today's Veterans and their families thrive back home on Main Street? Because our Federal systems are failing today's Veterans and it's up to us, "We the People." Main Street is the only safety net nimble enough to catch this generation of Veterans and their families. Each one of us must make a personal decision about what future we want for our military and their families coming home. We must make a personal decision about what future we want for our communities. And, we must decide whether we want to live with another 50 years of shame and stigma for how we treated our own people coming home from America's wars.

And, really, that's the way we've always done it as Americans.... from the pilgrims to the pioneers, from women's suffrage to the civil rights movement. It's how we survived the Great Depression, the bombing of Pearl Harbor and World War II. It's how we got Occupy Wall Street and the Tea Party movement. We didn't wait for Congress to pass laws. We didn't apply for Federal grants. As citizens, we saw a need, or we decided we didn't like how things were going, and we took action.

So, what if I told you that I could help you support our military coming home in a way that strengthens community, creates cost savings and economic development, and lays a foundation to rebuild America? Would you be interested? Would you join the movement? Because that's why I wrote this little book.

Yes, I am deeply alarmed by what is happening to America's more than three million post-9/11 Veterans, Guard, Reserve and their families. Yes, I am gravely worried about the long-term impact on Hometown America as we welcome our warriors home and shoulder the burden of care for them and their families. But, most importantly, I believe in the power of community and the resourcefulness of Americans on Main Street. It's time for us to stop looking to Washington for solutions. It's time for us, "We the People," to do what we have always done best: roll up our sleeves, solve our own problems, and take care of our own people.

I believe that in helping our military coming home, we can bridge the military-civilian divide, prevent the loss of another generation of Veterans, heal our communities from more than a decade at war, and lay the foundation to rebuild America in a way that embraces everyone and leaves us all proud.

As you read this little book, you will come to understand why we as a nation MUST work at the community level to bridge the military-civilian divide and the consequences if we fail to bridge the gap. You will learn what makes this generation of military different from our young Vietnam-era Veterans, why our Federal systems are not working better, and how these factors collude to hinder the successful transition for today's young military. Most importantly, you will discover concrete ways that you can help prevent America from losing another generation of military and their families.

We ALL have something at stake here. We may have misplaced some of the best parts of ourselves, but we have not completely lost our American values. It is not too late for us to reclaim what has always been one of America's greatest strengths: our ability to reinvent ourselves and our commitment to take care of our own. If enough Americans take the time to read this little book, I believe we can weave a community-based safety net for today's young military in transition and their families. In doing so, we will recapture a piece of ourselves and a piece of American culture that has been displaced by politics, economic stress, and more than a decade at war.

And, in asking our young Veterans to pay it forward, we will have rewritten our nation's social contract....a contract that bridges the military-civilian divide, prevents the loss of another generation of Veterans, and heals our communities from more than a decade at war.

With gratitude for all of those who serve our nation,
in uniform or not,

gretchen

P.S. As the founder of Homeward Deployed, many of the concepts and perspectives you will encounter here have shaped our programs. However, the views expressed here are entirely my own. They do not necessarily represent the views and perspectives of Homeward Deployed Board Members or staff.

THE MILITARY-CIVILIAN DIVIDE: PART ONE

WHY COMMUNITIES MUST MOBILIZE TO SUPPORT POST-9/11 MILITARY

Perhaps you have already decided to read this little book in its entirety, or perhaps you are skeptical that it is worth your time. Maybe you are asking yourself, "Why should I care about what is happening to our young post-9/11 military? It doesn't affect me or my life." Maybe you tell yourself, "I didn't want this war. I didn't vote for that president." If you'll humor me and finish this section, I will make the case for why you should care, or at least why you should be concerned and how it will, with nearly 100% certainty, affect you and your family. It's alarming, but there is hope and a host of solutions.

WHY THE 1% IS ACTUALLY 5%

The military has used the refrain "we are the 1%," meaning that only 1% of the population bears the burden of active duty service. Bear with me for two paragraphs while I make the case that the 1% is really more like 5%. And, that is an even greater cause for concern when we look at what is happening with our post-9/11 military.

As of 2012, America has about 2.2 million post-9/11 Veterans and more than 850,000 National Guard and Reservists. As we end the wars in the Middle East and enter the period of the drawdown (the military word for what we on Main Street call "downsizing"), the military is projecting a reduction its N-strength (what we call "number of employees") by as many as a million Service Members. So, by the time the drawdown is complete in 2016, America may well have more than 3.2 million post-9/11 Veterans back home on Main Street.

The average age of today's military is 29. Roughly 70% are under the age of 30; 50% are under the age of 25; and nearly 20% are 18 to 21. So, by 2020 many of these young Veterans will get married, if they are not already. And, they will have on average two children, if they have not already. Add to that the care-givers of the seriously wounded who will require care for the rest of their lives. Add to that the immediate families of the more than 6,000 killed in action, including spouses, partners, children, parents, and siblings. Add in the immediate families of our post-9/11 military who have taken their own lives. Suddenly, 3.2 million Veterans have now become more than 12 million post-9/11 Veteran families. With a U.S. population of over 314 million citizens, more than 4% of our population by 2020 will be post-9/11 military- affiliated. Voila! The 1% is really 5%.

A TSUNAMI OF NEED

So, over the next five years, we will have more than 3 million Veterans transitioning home to Main Street, plus our Guard and Reserve families. And, over a ten or twenty year time frame, they will bring with them an additional nine to ten million immediate family members who are also part of the transition process. What will that look like? Here's what we know in early 2013 about our 2.2 million post-9/11 Veterans (citations are found in the reference section; each issue is addressed more fully in the chapter called "Who Are America's Post-9/11 Military"):

- Roughly 50% of our post-9/11 Veterans report that they are not transitioning well
- 67% of our post-9/11 Veterans report that the needs of their families are not being met
- 200,000 Veterans have been diagnosed with Traumatic Brain Injuries but new screening techniques suggest that 19% of all post-9/11 Veterans may have some form of TBI
- More than 43,000 Service Members were injured in combat with an additional 55,000 injured in non-hostile environments
- Unemployment for National Guard averages 34%
- Estimates of the real unemployment rate for post-9/11 Veterans age 18-24 range as high as 31%

- 4% of post-9/11 Veterans experience homelessness and the number is rising, especially for female Veterans with children
- 22% of female and 14% of male Veterans report being diagnosed with Post-Traumatic Stress Disorder
- More than 52% of combat Veterans and 30% of non-combat Veterans report coping with emotional trauma
- More Service Members commit suicide annually than die in combat; the suicide rate among active duty Service Members has increased 18% in the last year
- It is estimated 26% of Service Members have mental health issues; half of them receive no treatment
- 27% of Service Members struggle with alcohol abuse, a 56% increase since 2003
- A female Service Member is more likely to be raped by her peer than she is to die in combat; 23% experience sexual assault and 67% experience sexual harassment
- Some reports place the student Veteran dropout rate as high as 88%, wasting billions of dollars in mis-spent GI Bill benefits
- Domestic abuse in military families has increased 30% in the past five years
- Child maltreatment in military families has increased 43% in the past five years and America's Promise has now identified military children as an at-risk population
- Violent crime among Veterans has increased 30% in the past five years and PTSD courts are springing up all over the country

A Vast Ocean of Potential

Here's what we also know about our post-9/11 military. They have huge potential and a wealth of skills that we desperately need in our communities. Many of our post-9/11 military went into the Service because of 9/11. They passionately believe in America, so much so that they are willing to die for us. And, they carry with them that spirit of service that has always defined America.

As we continue to struggle with terrorism, both domestic and foreign, in our own communities, who better to work in our city and county governments than Veterans? Those who served in combat are well-trained in security protocols and disaster management; they bring a well-honed sense of vigilance to the job in public safety, emergency management, transportation, and public works.

Regardless of their military occupation specialty (known as a MOS), today's military come home with leadership and teamwork skills, a strong work ethic, a willingness to take calculated risks, an openness to training, a can-do attitude, respect for chain of command, and acceptance that you must work your way up the ladder. These are the intangible skills most employers are desperate for. And, they are the skills that are difficult to teach.

As our city/county managers struggle with community engagement, who better to turn to than our military coming home? They understand leadership and teambuilding. They are defined by a spirit of service. As our Veterans come home and get established, they will become a valuable resource to engage and mobilize citizens in community projects.

But, they're going to need a little bit of support from us to reach their full potential back home.

THE COST OF CARE

So, what is it going to cost to address all of these needs? The Congressional Budget Office estimates that the care cost for our post-9/11 Veterans will exceed $5.5B annually by 2020. Linda Bilmes, co-author of The Three Trillion Dollar War, raised that estimate to $8.4B annually by 2020. She and Joseph Stiglitz, her co-author, estimate the total long-term care costs for this generation of Veterans exceeds $1T just in Federal entitlements.

One trillion dollars! That's a really big number. To give you an idea of what this means, and what's at stake....America has been grappling with how to solve the Social Security and Medicare crises for years. Every year, the deadline for these programs "going bankrupt" moves closer. Now, consider that we have a third ball to juggle, and it's just as big as Social Security and Medicare....it's called the long-term care costs for our post-9/11 Veterans. Oh, and we just entered sequestration. And, hating to be the bearer of more bad news, that number does not include the costs to our city and county governments in Hometown America where our Veterans actually live. These costs include extra dollars on Main Street for

- Housing services – homeless shelters, domestic violence shelters, Temporary Assistance to Needy Families (TANF), and low income housing
- Social services – domestic violence programs, substance abuse programs, foster care, benefits/case management, employment centers
- Health systems – mental health centers, clinics, ambulance services, and hospitals
- Student systems – daycare, Head Start, public K-12, after school programs, tutoring, libraries, parks and recreation programs, colleges and universities
- Justice systems – police departments, court systems, and jails

And, let me be clear here, this is not an issue of inherently "bad" Veterans. It is an issue of often very young people transitioning with inadequate support to successfully move forward. A person in transition, military or civilian, does not typically turn to negative support systems if they are offered a positive support system. But, in the absence of a productive pathway forward, they will turn to other systems of support, no matter how dysfunctional.

THE POWER OF PREVENTION

So, is there anything we can do avoid or minimize these costs? In short, yes....we can implement evidence-based prevention programs.

What this means is that we don't re-invent the wheel but that we look to research and existing programs to show us what is working. Then, we put money into those programs BEFORE disaster strikes. We are not a prevention-focused society, but now would be a really good time to start!

The rule of thumb is that for every $1 we put into prevention, we save $9 in remediation. Prevention saves money, it creates well-being, and it saves lives. So, does that mean that if we invest $1.1 billion we can prevent the entire $1 trillion long-term care bill for this generation of Veterans? No, that's ridiculous. There will absolutely be non-negotiable costs associated with taking care of our Veterans who fought America's wars. However, there is the potential to substantially reduce that bill by smart investing in solid programs....immediately and in spite of the economy. We can pay $1 for a pound of prevention now, or pay $9 later for a pound of cure. And, in the gap, Veterans will commit suicide, parents will divorce, and children will be harmed.

By helping young Veterans, Guard, Reserve and their families transition well, we build sustainability through a productive work force and an engaged citizenry. Everybody wins. Sounds simple, doesn't it? And, in some ways, it is.

More Bad News: Help Isn't Coming

I'm sorry to share this but there is one more piece of bad news. Help is not coming from our Federal Agencies, as you will see in the chapter called "The Big Picture." It is not the mission of the Department of Defense to handle Veteran issues. The Department of Veterans Affairs is overwhelmed by the demand for services. The Department of Labor is struggling to find effective solutions. Congress is at war with itself. The Veterans Opportunity to Work (VOW) Act is largely an unfunded mandate. Hometown America, we're on our own. And, the sooner we accept this, the sooner we can move towards prevention-based solutions. What we resist persists.

So, here's the deal, Mr. and Mrs. America. Good or bad, right or wrong, fair or unfair, the burden of care for this generation of Veterans and their families is going to fall on Main Street. Our military coming home are not simply going to stay at Fort Hood or Camp Pendleton forever. That's why they call it "coming HOME."

But, is it really our responsibility, you may challenge me? Here's the deal with responsibility....break the word apart and you get response-ability, the ability to respond. As you will see shortly, the ONLY system we have left that has the ABILITY to respond quickly enough to PREVENT this tsunami is COMMUNITY. And, every study of powerful, permanent community change shows that it comes from the bottom up, from We the People, the citizens and leaders of Main Street.

This is not an issue of patriotism but an issue of the financial and human consequences of failure to respond. Remember, we pay now or we pay later, but eventually we will pay. I realize that Main Street is suffering the brunt of the recession....I am a civilian who lives on Main Street myself. But, it doesn't mean we don't have options. What has always made America strong is our ability to overcome challenges and reinvent ourselves. What we have always done best is to work together to solve our own problems. That is the true power of community. WE CAN DO THIS....if we put our minds to it.

At a very deep level, it is an issue of who we want to be as an American people. Why do we fight? We fight for our families and our communities, for our quality of life, for other families we want to enjoy those same freedoms. Do we want to be a society that sends our young people to war and then welcomes them home by sitting back and watching them fail? Did that serve us after Vietnam?

What does America mean to you? What kind of America do you want for your children and grandchildren? Are you willing to entrust this future to Washington? Or, are you willing to fight to take back the best parts of ourselves, pieces that have been misplaced by the stresses of ten years of war and a global economic meltdown? I truly hope your answer is, "yes."

THE MILITARY-CIVILIAN DIVIDE: PART TWO

WHAT THE MILITARY NEEDS TO UNDERSTAND ABOUT MAIN STREET

Some of you reading this little book may be from the military yourselves or a military-affiliated family member. There are, after all, more than 23 million Veterans in America, most of whom come attached to family. Some of the things that I am going to say here may be hard for you to hear. They may make you angry. But, bridging the military-civilian divide is not just about civilians understanding military culture and reaching out to you. You need to understand us and meet us half way. It's called the art of compromise, where both sides often need to address inconvenient truths and neither side gets everything they want...but, ideally, everyone gets what they need and society is the better for it.

OUR RELATIONSHIP WITH THE FEDERAL GOVERNMENT

Many citizens of Main Street feel like our President and Congress have forgotten us. Politics has become so polarized that nothing seems to get done. In Hometown America, Congress seems more like "by the rich, for the rich" than "by the people, for the people." Wall Street gets bailouts and then posts record profits while we lose our jobs, spend our retirement savings trying to get by, and fall into foreclosure on our homes. The President hosts lavish parties and takes trips to Martha's Vineyard when we can't afford to eat at Outback Steakhouse or take the kids on a weekend trip to the beach.

For the first time since Vietnam, the U.S. Conference of Mayors passed a resolution in June 2011 to "bring the war dollars home." As citizens, we read about the $3 TRILLION (wow, that is a big number) our Federal leaders have authorized on the war, a number that keeps increasing. And while we are fully funding the global war on terror, Main Street is hemorrhaging. Our tax dollars fund state of the art hospitals to treat Veterans, hospitals to which we have no access, at a cost of as much as $1 billion; meanwhile, hospitals on Main Street can't afford to repair, replace, or purchase basic equipment like MRIs. As the Army addresses a $5 billion "mistake" in its uniforms and prepares to spend another $5 billion on new uniforms, again paid for by our tax dollars, millions of unemployed and underemployed Americans and their children are foregoing new clothes entirely.

Good or bad, right or wrong, fair or unfair, you work for a Federal agency and, sometimes, to us, you represent the Federal system that has abandoned us. This leaves us feeling really conflicted. We do not want to recreate what happened to our Vietnam Veterans. We work to separate the war from the warrior. But, sometimes the unfairness of it all gets a bit too much to take. Why did the Tea Party spring into existence? Where did Occupy Wall Street come from? We feel like no one is listening to us. We feel like no one cares. We feel alone. I'm guessing you do, too. Perhaps we have common ground here?

JOBS, HEALTH CARE, AND EDUCATION

As Chair of the Joint Staff, Admiral Mullen created a model for Veteran transition based on jobs, health care, and education. Organizations like Iraq and Afghanistan Veterans of America have been very effective in advocacy, lobbying, and getting legislation passed around these three issues. Literally thousands of nonprofits are reaching out to Veterans and their families. And, that's great for our military and their affiliates. But what about those of us who come from Main Street? We feel like Cinderella, except that the prince never arrives.

We aren't happy that nearly a million Veterans, Guard, and Reserve are unemployed or underemployed. But, we aren't really happy that there are 13 million unemployed or underemployed civilians either. We try to be happy for you that the White House, Congress, and corporate America are bending over backwards to help you find jobs. But, sometimes, we ask, "What about us?" We know your rate of unemployment is higher (9.5% versus 8.2%) but our numbers are 13 times higher. We see all the resources being focused on helping you find jobs. We see all the Veteran preferences. And, sometimes, we feel resentful. We feel overlooked. In spite of how much we care, it feels unfair.

Between 2007 and 2010, the wealth of middle class families dropped 39%, eliminating two decades of prosperity. Our median family income dropped 8%. In recent years, many of us have had to raid our retirement funds just to keep a roof over our heads and food on the table. Meanwhile, from 2001 to 2012, military pay increased 20%, paid by our tax dollars which directly impacts our daily financial lives. How would you feel if you were on the other side of the military-civilian divide? Can you see how it would be hard for us to be sympathetic to your calls for pay raises and protests against revising the military retirement system?

We know you have been through a lot with the multiple cycles of deployment. We know that there are hundreds of thousands of wounded Veterans from the current wars. But, when you advocate so ferociously for expanded health care for Veterans, and Congress passes your bills, we wonder if you know that there are between 45 and 50 million people without health insurance in the U.S.? That's roughly 17% of the population. When you can get disability for life because you got an injury playing football while deployed or because you developed diabetes while on active duty, we wonder if you understand that when those things happen to civilians on Main Street we get absolutely nothing. And, those injuries and illnesses may make us permanently uninsurable unless we work for a company that has group health insurance. Even with great health, it can cost $400 a month for a 50 year old to private pay for an HMO. Can you understand how it can be hard for us to empathize when you get so much and we pay the bills through our tax dollars for your benefits, benefits which many of us are denied ourselves?

We know that many of you went into the military to earn GI Bill benefits. Then we read that 88% of Veterans drop out and only 3% of

Veterans ever graduate (yes, these are highly controversial numbers, I'm a statistics gal, but bear with me). American taxpayers have spent more than $18 billion to send you to college, and now it looks like we have wasted almost all of it. Even if the numbers are lower, we've still mis-spent a lot of money. Meanwhile, our children have accumulated nearly $1 trillion dollars of debt in student loans. Can you see how we would be angry and resentful that we pay your tuition bills and many of you squander the opportunity, while our children are saddled with a lifetime of debt?

So, sometimes, it feels to us like you really aren't part of Main Street because you have so many resources directed your way, resources and benefits paid for by us to you, when we get none of those same benefits. Many of you misuse the benefits we pay for on your behalf. So, sometimes we feel taken advantage of. Often, we feel like no one cares about the 95%. We feel forgotten, abandoned, and invisible. Perhaps we have common ground here?

YOU PUSH US AWAY

And, when we do try to mobilize our communities to support you, often you push us away. You tell us that we don't understand military culture, but you won't take the time to talk to us and share your experiences so that we can understand. Military leadership tells us that you don't need our help, that they have it handled. How many times do you think we want to reach out only to have the door slammed in our faces? Often, you make us feel unwelcome, so we stop trying to reach out.

You tell us we can't understand your experiences with combat, with Post-Traumatic Stress, with the constant moves, with the pressure on your marriages and your families. While we haven't been in combat, we are exposed to trauma and violence through our jobs as police officers, EMTs, emergency room physicians, defense contractors, social workers, and nonprofit employees in high crime communities. We, too, are victims of domestic abuse and sexual assault. We have had marriages fall apart from the stresses of job loss, illness, foreclosure, disability, and the death of a child. When you tell us we cannot understand your experiences, you devalue us and you prevent us from finding common ground that bridges the military-civilian divide. Just food for thought.

We Serve, Too

The issue of service is a tricky one. We know that many of America's Veterans, Guard, and Reserve have served in combat. We can only imagine or read about what you have been through. We are not oblivious to the scars, both physical and mental, that you will carry with you for the rest of your lives. And, we recognize that this impacts not just you but your families as well.

However, many of us serve America, too. We just don't wear combat boots. We are America's teachers, nurses, attendants in assisted living facilities, nonprofit staff, beat officers, EMTs, and fire fighters. Many of us donate hundreds of hours at Veteran serving organizations for no pay. And, many of us are in harm's way on Main Street because we work in high crime neighborhoods, or we work with criminals or people with serious mental health issues, or we're exposed to people with hepatitis or AIDS.

And, about the flag, that's another touchy issue for all of us. But, it needs to be said....the American flag does not just belong to those who defended it in combat. Legions of lawyers, journalists, elected officials, and leaders on Main Street strive to uphold our shared democratic ideals and the tenets of the Constitution. Martin Luther King Jr., Harvey Milk, Leo Ryan, Huey Long, James Davis, Bill Gwatney, Derwin Brown, Chauncy Bailey, and Gabriel Giffords paid high prices in service to the flag and the ideals it stands for. (Don't feel badly if you don't recognize all the names, I had to do some research myself!) So, when you say that we owe you because of your service to America, ignoring the fact that many of us serve in our own ways....when you claim to have exclusive rights to patriotism....it makes us angry. It's insulting. And, underneath the anger, we feel devalued by you for our contributions to making America a better place to live. Can we agree that we all love America and want to see it prosper?

What about what civilians need to understand about the military? This is the purpose of the rest of the book! We have our homework ahead of us.

THE BIG PICTURE: PART ONE

HOW THIS WAR IS DIFFERENT FROM VIETNAM AND THE GULF WAR

Many issues divided America during the sixties and early seventies. U.S. Soldiers fought communists in Vietnam while hippies got high at Woodstock. The battle for equal rights for Black Americans was fought on the streets of Selma and in Saigon. And, in spite of the fact that young men were drafted and had no option to military service, beyond fleeing to Canada, they came home to anti-war protests, animosity, and accusations.

While 9/11 brought our nation together for a brief period of time, a decade later we are as divided as we were during Vietnam over issues of abortion, gay rights, immigration, and economic inequality. Ironically, although our post-9/11 military is an all-volunteer force of Service Members who choose to fight, Americans from all walks of life have worked very hard to separate the war from the warrior.

So, this can make it hard to understand why our post-9/11 Veterans, Guard, and Reserve are having so much trouble transitioning. America learned its lessons from Vietnam and we now welcome our Soldiers home, so what's the problem? Why aren't they thriving? In the next few paragraphs, I will explain what I see as the critical differences between these two wars and how they are impacting our post-9/11 military.

SOLDIERS KILLED IN ACTION

More than 3 million Americans served in Vietnam and roughly 695,000 in Desert Storm. By the time we reach the end of the drawdown, America will have more than 3 million post-9/11 Service Members. America suffered a terrible loss of life in Vietnam, with 55,220 killed in action; this compares to 383 killed during Desert Storm and 6549 killed post-9/11. The significant reduction in loss of life between the wars is attributed to the dramatic improvements in battlefield and emergency medicine. But the terrible loss of life during Vietnam is balanced by the extraordinary rate of injury for our post-9/11 military.

One of two significant differences between Vietnam and our wars in Iraq and Afghanistan are the number of casualties. While the majority of soldiers seriously wounded in combat in Vietnam died, the majority of soldiers seriously wounded in combat post-9/11 are still alive today.

In Vietnam, America suffered roughly 150,000 casualties (total) with 21,000 permanently disabled. Desert Storm produced 467 casualties. Our post-9/11 wars have seen more than 48,000 wounded in theater with more than 244,000 confirmed Traumatic Brain Injuries, although some studies place that number at over 400,000. This number will continue to increase until all of our Service Members are out of Iraq and Afghanistan.

And, then, there are the invisible or mental wounds of war. Approximately 830,000 Vietnam-era Veterans, or 28%, have been diagnosed with Post-traumatic Stress (PTSD). It is estimated that 15% of post-9/11 Veterans at any given time, will be managing PTSD, with an accumulated lifetime incidence of 30%, or nearly 1 million. Some have placed those numbers at 40% or 50%, or higher.

To give you a mental picture of what our nation is facing in long-term care for our post-9/11 Veterans, imagine the Vietnam Veterans Memorial in Washington DC (also known as "The Wall") where the name of every Soldier killed in Vietnam is etched. Now imagine that wall six to eight times in height. That is the wall we must scale as a nation if we are going to heal the visible and invisible wounds of our post-9/11 warriors.

The second significant difference between Vietnam and our wars in Iraq and Afghanistan are the number of deployments. Because we no longer have a draft, America relies on a much smaller number of Service Members to fight our wars. During Vietnam, we had roughly 8.7 million Service Members worldwide, with 3.4 million serving in southeast Asia. Since 9/11, we have had roughly 2.3 million Service members worldwide, 2.2 million of whom served in Iraq and Afghanistan.

Significant U.S. military presence in Vietnam lasted roughly ten years. The vast majority of soldiers were deployed for a single 12 month tour of duty. The entire Gulf War lasted just seven months, with single tours of duty lasting no more than 7 months.

By contrast, our post-9/11 wars have dragged on for more than 11 years, with the U.S. maintaining troops in Iraq and Afghanistan into 2014. Average deployments last between 12 and 15 months. And, multiple deployments are common, with 31% of troops deploying twice, 12% deploying three times, and 4% deploying four times or more. These figures are from January 2010 so the real numbers are likely much higher and will continue to rise until our troop are all home from Iraq and Afghanistan.

THE ECONOMY

While our Vietnam Era Veterans came home to animosity, they returned to an economy on Main Street that was enjoying its longest period of uninterrupted expansion in America's history. While hippies and college students protested the war, it was World War II and Korean War Veterans who ran America's businesses and hired our returning Vietnam Veterans.

Our post-9/11 Veterans have come home to the worst economic downturn since America's Great Depression. Hometown America has worked to separate the war from the warrior and welcome home our Veterans, Guard, and Reserve. However, with the end of the draft in 1973 and the transition to an all-volunteer force, most of America's business owners today have no military experience themselves. The combination of a battered economy and a majority of employers who don't understand military experience or resumes, has made successful employment transition for America's post-9/11 Veterans even harder. The challenges of employment transition will be covered later.

THE BIG PICTURE: PART TWO

In working on military transition issues since 2006, I have found that many people in Hometown America don't understand why our Federal agencies don't seem to do more. Quite frankly, it took me a while to figure it out. And, this is a key piece to understanding why it is so important for communities to mobilize to support our Veterans and why help will not be coming from our Federal agencies.

UNDERSTANDING THE FEDERAL MILITARY HIERARCHY

The Department of Defense is the umbrella agency under which you find the Joint Chiefs of Staff, Department of the Army, Department of the Navy, and the Department of the Air Force. The Marine Corps Command falls under the Department of the Navy. The U.S. Coast Guard, while a military agency, falls under the Department of Homeland Security. That's another story!

There are two branches of the National Guard, Army and Air Force; their leadership falls under their respective Departments. There are five branches of the Reserves (Army, Navy, Marine, Air Force, Coast Guard), each falling under their respective Department.

And, within each agency, there are strict hierarchies and fierce competition between the services. Just think of the Army-Navy football game writ large. No wonder services aren't coordinated.

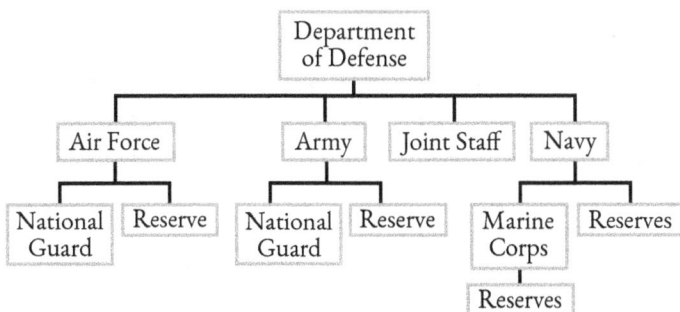

Many Americans believe that the Department of Defense (DoD) holds the primary responsibility to support our military in transition. However, the mission of the Department of Defense, which you can find on their website, is to "provide the military forces needed to deter war and to protect the security of our country." Supporting military in transition is a part of that mission only as it affects recruitment, retention, force readiness, and unit cohesion. Once you get your DD214 (your military retirement papers) and become a Veteran, you are no longer under the control of the DoD or their responsibility. Think of it like graduating. Once you get your diploma, your high school or college may have an interest in what happens to you, they may try to provide a few follow-up services, but their primary responsibility is to their enrolled students. It's not that they don't care, but the time has come for you to put on your big boy/girl pants and move out into the world, whether you are ready or not.

So, it is absolutely NOT the case that DoD leadership doesn't care. It's that they can't take action. The only way for the DoD to get a budget approved that focuses substantial funds towards Veteran transition would be for Congress to change its mission. With a Congress so divided they can't agree on tax code, you can only imagine what it would take to change the official mission of the Department of Defense, whose roots precede the American Revolution! George Washington would roll over in his grave!

That said, Admiral Michael Mullen, the former Chair of the Joint Chiefs of Staff made heroic efforts within the limitations set by his position, to support military in transition. He created the Office of Warrior Family Support and commissioned the "Sea of Goodwill" papers to encourage communities to work to support their military families. He sent Colonel David Sutherland on a national tour to meet and work with communities. And, he was instrumental in taking a brave stand in a divided America to end "Don't Ask, Don't Tell," beginning the process of creating dignity, respect, and equal rights within the military for America's 80,000+ gay Soldiers who fight in combat alongside their straight brothers and sisters. More on that later.

So, if it's not the mission of the DoD, then surely it must be the mission of the VA? After all, it is the Department of VETERANS Affairs!

The mission of the VA is to "to fulfill President Lincoln's promise to care for him who shall have borne the battle, and for his widow, and his orphan, by serving and honoring the men and women who are America's veterans." (A bit of trivia: While the VA was formally established after the Civil War to help those disabled in the war, the VA has its roots with the pilgrims who in 1636 agreed to care for soldiers injured in defending the Colonists from the Indians. Now you're ready for Jeopardy.)

The work of the VA is to administer Veteran benefits, provide vocational and rehabilitative services to disabled Veterans, and manage America's military cemeteries. And, herein lies the rub of it. You are only eligible for VA services IF you have been approved for those services. What many American's don't understand is that not all Veterans qualify for all services. It's a very complex web of formulas and entitlements which I don't begin to pretend to understand. So, many but not all Veterans are eligible for GI Bill benefits, and the level of benefits can vary widely. Vocational, rehabilitative, and employment services are only available for disabled Veterans with rated (verified) disabilities; and the level of benefits ranges from approval for a few physical therapy sessions to full disability pay for life.

Secretary Shinseki has made valiant efforts to improve the speed and quality of services at the VA but many Veterans will tell you that dysfunction at the VA goes back to the 1960s; Secretary Shinseki truly has his work cut out for him. Simply put, the VA is still overwhelmed. No one expected America to be at war for more than a decade with more than 3 million Veterans impacted. No one predicted the number and severity of injuries we would see as a result of Improvised Explosive Devices (IEDs) or the epidemic of mental health issues that have emerged as a result of multiple deployments.

As of early 2013, the VA had nearly 1 million claims backlogged, 66% of which had been pending more than 125 days. Some Veterans have documented a 600 day wait for services. Veterans seeking services are often advised to expect to wait two years for processing and access to services. An appeals process can take up to five years. This backlog has been complicated by changes for Vietnam Veterans around entitlements for exposure to Agent Orange, adding more than 250,000 new claims from our Vietnam Veterans in the past year. And, with the economy still struggling to recover, many Veterans are seeking services to fill gaps caused by unemployment and losses to their retirement portfolios.

Further complicating the picture for Veteran transition, roughly 70% of Veterans refuse to seek care at the VA, increasing the burden on state and local agencies and organizations. Women Veterans have traditionally been less likely to feel welcome at VA hospitals; this situation was made worse by a Congressional Report documenting 300 rapes in VA hospitals. It's gotten so bad that an underground, alternative motto has developed for the VA, "Delay, Deny and Hope That I Die." This is clearly not what most American taxpayers imagine as we pay our taxes to provide services for our Veterans. You could argue that we pay twice for care for America's Veterans....once in Federal taxes for inadequate VA care and again in state/local taxes for care on Main Street.

DEPARTMENT OF LABOR VETERAN EMPLOYMENT AND TRAINING SERVICE (DoL VETS)

The U.S. Department of Labor Veteran Employment and Training Service (DoL VETS) provides resources to assist Veterans to find meaningful careers and to protect Veteran employment rights. They have been actively working to address the issues of Veteran unemployment, most notably through their partnership with the U.S. Chamber of Commerce Hiring Our Heroes initiative. But, as with the rest of the DoL, their work is hampered by a challenging economy and high unemployment, factors over which they have no control.

DoL VETS also holds primary responsibility for designing and implementing the Transition Assistance Program (TAP) for transitioning military, although the DoD has significant input. The redesign and potential for this program is discussed in "The Big Picture, Part Three."

THE BIG PICTURE: PART THREE

UNDERSTANDING THE NATURE OF TRANSITION AND THE TRANSITION
ASSISTANCE PROGRAM (TAP)

The Transition Assistance Program (TAP) was designed in the 1990s with the goal of providing transition assistance before Veterans separate from the service, so that they seamlessly enter the civilian job market. The program is typically three days long and participation is not mandatory. TAP often takes active duty Service Members away from their duty stations, so their commanding officers often do not encourage participation. This is especially true for soldiers who are separating from the service immediately upon return from deployment, where taking virtual TAP takes them away from combat duty stations. Service Members generally have not found the program helpful, and it has developed such a poor reputation that fewer and fewer Service Members voluntarily enroll. In July 2012, a redesigned TAP was announced: Transition GPS, which must be fully implemented by November 2013.

TRANSITION GPS

The goal of Transition GPS is to support Service Members in successfully transitioning not just into the civilian workforce but also into starting a business or pursuing higher education. Unlike TAP, Transition GPS is mandatory, unless a Service Member has a job offer in hand, is returning to run an established business, or has been accepted into a college or training program.

Lasting five days instead of three, participants will attend trainings on financial planning, VA benefits and services, and finding employment. Participants will take assessments and receive one-to-one counseling with the goal of coming up with a concrete individual transition plan. In addition, participants may attend optional two-day workshops focused on pursuing a college degree, entering a technical skills training program, or starting a business.

The most innovative part of Transition GPS is the "Military Life Cycle Transition Model." This model incorporates career readiness and transition preparation into the lifespan of a Service Member's career, from the time they enlist until they separate from the Service. As a Service Member progresses in his/her career, they will focus on ensuring that they are gaining the skills and credentials they need to transition smoothly to civilian employment. This will have a tremendous impact on today's Service Members who remain in the Service as well as future Service Members. However, it offers nothing to those already out of the military, or those who are about to lose their jobs as a part of the drawdown.

I wish I could say that I have high hopes for Transition GPS and its supporting programs; instead I have serious concerns that it will not be any more effective than TAP. Please understand that this is not intended to diminish the efforts of our Federal agencies. But, there are some serious design flaws which speak to the need for Main Street to mobilize. If we assume that Transition GPS will magically solve the issue of Veteran transition for our post-9/11 military, our response on Main Street time will be further delayed and the likelihood of losing another generation of Veterans and their families will be increased.

The Period of Decompression

The greatest flaw I see with TAP and Transition GPS is timing. When a Service Member separates from the service and especially when they return home from deployment, they need time to "decompress"....in essence to "chill out," reconnect with family and friends, and process their experiences. For many of our active duty Service Members, return from deployment coincides with separation from the service. This will become increasingly true as the rate of the drawdown increases. While there is general recognition among military leadership of the importance of the decompression period, TAP and Transition GPS are and will always be positioned BEFORE decompression. Unfortunately, when transitioning military need transition support is AFTER they have decompressed, by which time they are typically home on Main Street. In other words, military transition happens on Main Street. So, if the DoD cannot provide real-time services on Main Street, then Hometown America is going to have to step up or decide to sit back and watch another generation of Veterans and their families fail. It's not fair, but it is the reality.

Transition is Not a Five Day Event

Coming from civilian communities into military culture, military leaders recognized the need for intensive training and they created boot camp. Boot camp for newly enlisted Service Members is an intensive, highly structured three to four month transition process. During boot camp, Service Members receive all the training, skills, and resources they need to be effective in their military occupational specialty. Think about it....our post-9/11 military spent 90 to 120 days making the transition into the military. Do we really think 5 days is sufficient to help them transition back home, especially after multiple deployments?

Consider America's young enlisted who often transition into the military straight out of high school. When they transition out, they may have never lived outside the structure of the military. They were given a job and a uniform; they were told where to live, when to eat, where to shop, how to exercise, and where to go for medical care. When our young enlisted come home, they lack experience not just in writing resumes, interviewing, networking, and figuring out how to dress but experience in basic life skills like acquiring housing, obtaining health insurance, finding doctors, evaluating schools, and building community relationships from scratch.

Now consider our retiring Service Members, say the master sergeant in charge of supply chain. He spent 20 years or more in the military and his identity has been defined by his military occupational specialty. He knew exactly how to act by reading the rank on a person's chest. While he has defended America and its ideals, often in combat, and while he and his family may have lived on Main Street, they were defined by military culture. Now, they are no longer a part of that culture, and the transition to civilian life may be a bit of culture shock.

Now imagine you were an 88mike (transportation) or an 11bravo (infantry). You are transitioning out because you are a victim of the drawdown. You are angry at being downsized and you are scared about how you are going to survive. You have no idea what you want to do with your life, except that you do know you don't want a civilian career as a long-haul truck driver or a security officer at the mall. You're thinking about using your GI Bill benefits to go back to school but your wife wants you to get a job so that you can have another baby, something you delayed due to multiple deployments. And, in addition to balancing your needs with a wife and child, you may be managing a disability or caring for elderly parents. Are you going to create a life plan in five days with an hour or two of counseling?

The White House has described this process as "reverse boot camp," but no one in any walk of life "reverses" years of life experience. What we do is use our experiences to learn and grow as we move forward. This is the genesis of Homeward Deployed's Transition Boot Camp, which incorporates an individual's military experience and works to support that individual in integrating military experience so that they can create a "new normal" and identify new goals that pull them onto a pathway of economic stability and family resilience. Achieving this kind of transition readiness is not a five day event. And, it happens on Main Street. No, it's not fair, but it is the reality.

Online Tools

In response to the needs of transitioning Service Members, Guard, and Reserve, a multitude of online tools have been developed....websites, webinars, YouTube videos, even a version of TAP called "eTAP" that consists of a series of PowerPoint presentations. Now, ask yourself, when you were in crisis or transition, what did you do? Did you power up your computer or smart phone to google websites? Did you click through a set of generic PowerPoint slides?

Or, did you reach out to a human being....your partner or spouse, a friend, your mom or dad, a brother or sister, your pastor, a co-worker? Human beings transition and heal in the company of other caring human beings. If this were not true, Sigmund Freud would have written a book on transition and when we graduated from high school, we all would get a copy. When we hit a crisis or transition point, we would read the appropriate chapter and voila! We would be fine. But, the existence of the fields of psychology, clinical social work, and coaching tells us people do not heal and transition via books, brochures, websites, tele-classes, or Powerpoints. Human relationships are required. And, those human relationships will be formed on Main Street. Some Veterans will have strong family structures but many will not, and as community members we will need to step in. No, it's not fair, but it is the reality. And, if you have ever reached out a hand to someone, you know that often you get more out of it than they do. And, if you have ever had someone help you, this is an excellent time to pay it forward.

The Problem with Job Fairs

You have probably seen media coverage of the multitude of Veteran Job Fairs. Here's the rub of it: they don't work. For example, the U.S. Chamber of Commerce Hiring Our Heroes Job Fairs report producing 10,000 jobs but that constitutes an 8% success rate given that they have had 120,000 participants in these job fairs. Furthermore, the reality is that participants walk away with an invitation to a job interview not a job. No hiring managers I know actually make firm job commitments via a 20 minute chat at a job fair.

These high profile job fairs disproportionately have employers from the Fortune 500 and Wall Street. This is a great venue if you are an officer with a college or graduate degree and a security clearance. However, if you are an 88mike or an 11bravo or a military spouse with a high school degree, there are not many jobs that you qualify for in the Fortune 500.

Finally, small businesses with fewer than 500 employees account for 99.7% of jobs and more than 70% of job creation. So, if Veterans are going to find jobs, it is going to be in small companies not the Fortune 500. Small businesses hire predominantly by word-of-mouth not at large job fairs or via Monster; the rule of thumb is that only 5% of people find jobs by submitting resumes online or via job postings. So, if our post-9/11 Veterans are not attending community chamber of commerce mixers or other business oriented events where small business owners network, they are not going to meet prospective employers. This is a tremendous opportunity for both Veterans and community members to create bridges to employment, as you will see in the chapter "How Can I Help?"

The Issue with Tax Credits

Tax credits may seem like a great idea but, like anything associated with tax code, they can be difficult to implement and take advantage of. For large businesses, the maximum tax per Veteran hired is $9,600 for a service-disabled Veteran who has been out of work at least six months and earns no more than $24,000 per year. Many large businesses believe that it is not worth the trouble for such a small amount of money. For small businesses, who could really benefit in a down economy from the ability to hire a competent staff member at just over 50% salary, the reporting requirements are so great that they typically cannot pursue the tax credits for lack of adequate accounting and staffing help. So, if tax credits are going to be effective, then they must either give a greater tax benefit or simplify the reporting process, or both.

The Challenge of Veteran Entrepreneurship

Veteran entrepreneurship is a very small part of the picture but it is being heavily pushed as an alternative to traditional employment. Those of you who are business owners know that it is simply not true that owning your own business is easier than having a "real job." A two day workshop taken in the middle of a major life transition will never prepare anyone with the solid business plan or necessary skills to run a profitable business. The rule of thumb in today's economy is that it takes five years to establish a stable business; roughly 80% of new businesses fail within three years. So, entrepreneurship is not likely to prove a realistic pathway for young Veterans, Guard, or Reserve who must have immediate or short-term income stability. Our young transitioning military are often lured by the promise of low interest Patriot Express business loans, reduced franchising fees, preferences when it comes to government contracting, and the Hollywood image of what it takes to be a successful business owner. This sets our Veterans and their families up for a cycle of failure, not a cycle of success.

The "Warm Handover"

Finally, Transition GPS depends on a "warm handover" for Veterans who leave the program still not "Career Ready." Admiral Mullen laid out a framework for a structure to provide this "warm handover." Joining Forces, out of the White House, advocates for this structure. Army Community Covenant facilitates agreements between military and civilian communities to work together to build this structure. The Community Blueprint is working on a model to support the self-mobilization at the community level to create this structure, but to date there are fewer than 50 Blueprint communities out of more than 19,000 municipalities.

So, as we enter the drawdown and communities struggle to integrate as many as one million new Veterans in the next three years, many of whom are leaving the military against their will, help is not coming. American communities will need to choose to self-engage, self-mobilize, and take self-responsibility. Or, we need to choose to let our post-9/11 Veterans figure out their transition alone. And, we all know how well that worked after Vietnam. For the last time, no, it's not fair, but it is the reality.

WHO ARE AMERICA'S POST-9/11 MILITARY?

There are literally millions of people in America's post-9/11 military community. This chapter is intended to help you understand the scope and breadth of this community as well as some key issues facing them.

ACTIVE DUTY SERVICE MEMBERS

	Total	Enlisted	Officer
Rank	1.4M+	84%	16%
Women	14%	14%	16%
Minorities	30%	87%	13%
Have HS Diploma/GED	80%	94%	7%
Have BA or Higher	20%	10%	90%
Average Age	29	27	35
Under 25	44%	50%	13%
Under 30	66%	72%	36%
Living outside the U.S.	17%	n/a	n/a

America's active duty Service Members are 39% Army, 23% Air Force, 22% Navy, 14% Marine Corps, and 3% Coast Guard. These active duty Service Members are young. Roughly two thirds are under the age of 30, half are under the age of 25, and nearly 20% are 18 to 21. Roughly 84% are enlisted. Most enlisted enter the military right out of high school so the structure of military culture is the only life they know as adults. As they transition out, many will lack the basic life skills and family relationships they need to transition well, especially those who come from America's underserved and rural communities.

I met "Joe" when I served on an employer panel at a Marine transition program. Joe grew up in Kentucky coal mining country. He enlisted in the Marine Corps right out of high school and served four years as a file clerk.

He was lucky to come home to strong family support. His father, brothers, and uncles where anxious for him to join them in the coal mines.

But, Joe wanted to be a teacher. While his family loved him, they had trouble understanding why he didn't want to work in the mines. No one in his community had ever been to college. Who would help Joe to figure out his GI Bill benefits, apply to college, adapt to campus life, and succeed academically? While the military may help Joe get his GI Bill benefits, he will look to the systems of Main Street to help him figure the rest out. If those systems fail him, Main Street may lose a valuable community asset— an educator with a genuine commitment to serve.

Pay grades for enlisted are determined by rank (E-1 to E-9) and number of years in the service. In 2012, a first year E-1 earned $17,892. An E-9 with over 20 years of service earned $66,283. Service Members get a housing allowance, which can range from $7,056 for an unmarried E-1 in Alabama to $38,664 for a married E-9 with dependents in San Francisco. Additionally, Service Members and their families are entitled to healthcare, life insurance, disability insurance, free access to exercise and other recreation facilities, reduced cost for high quality child care on base, and discounts at the commissary (military grocery store) and exchange (military department store). So, a young enlisted may have a salary and benefits equivalent to $30,000 or $40,000. This compensation level can be very difficult if not impossible to recreate back home on Main Street with a high school diploma or GED, especially in today's economy.

While some enlisted will earn certifications or college degrees while in the Service, most will not. This is changing with the implementation of Transition GPS, but it will not help most of America's post-9/11 Veterans. So, as we move through the five year period of the drawdown, many enlisted will return home to Main Street with skills that do not easily translate to civilian occupations. And, their expectations for salary and benefits are not realistic for a civilian economy hemorrhaging after three years of economic instability.

"Miguel" was referred to Homeward Deployed through a board member. Miguel served as an air traffic controller on aircraft carriers and intended to make the Navy his career, like his father before him. He developed a medical condition which made him undeployable and he was medically retired from the Navy after ten years of service, leaving him ineligible for a military pension. His medical condition prevented him from pursuing a career as a civilian air traffic controller. He was 29 with a high school degree, two daughters from previous relationships, and heavy child-support commitments which he always met on time. Having nowhere to go, he moved in with his parents, in a community where he had never lived before. He eventually found employment managing a Radio Shack in a local mall, at half his Navy pay with no benefits.

Miguel's transition assistance had failed him. Fortunately, Main Street did not. Miguel was motivated to make a better life for himself and his daughters. The Board member saw something in Miguel, and so did his coach. You see, it turns out that Miguel only made it halfway through management training at Radio Shack before he was put in charge of the highest volume store in his community of a million people....with no retail or traditional management experience. That was his marketable skill. Within two months, Miguel was able to transition into a sales position at a local company, recreating his Navy salary. Miguel now has a bright future, especially if he decides to go back to school. Sadly, Miguel's success is not shared by many of today's transitioning enlisted.

Military officer pay in 2012 ranged from $42,703 for an O-1 with four years of service to $112,440 for an O-6 (Colonel) with twenty years of service to $187,765 for an 0-10 (General) plus benefits. While officers absolutely go through a transition period, a college educated officer with a security clearance is in very high demand in the defense industry. They typically have far more life experience and resources to draw on in order to successfully transition.

Nearly 200,000 active duty Service Members separate from the service each year. The Department of Labor VETS estimates this number will increase to 300,000 each year from 2013 to 2016 as we end the wars and enter the drawdown. Involuntary separations from the service—for issues of behavior, performance, and legal entanglements—account for a surprising 29% of all separations; 98% of Service Members who were involuntarily separated were enlisted. No research is available to show how many of these involuntary separations are ultimately the result of untreated mental health issues or undiagnosed mild brain injuries, but I would suspect that it may account for a substantial proportion. Involuntary separation often means that a Service Member leaves the service with no benefits or access to transition services, adding disproportionately to the burden of care faced by Hometown America.

> "Melissa" was a young Veteran spouse with a toddler; she had a high school diploma and was a stay-at-home mom. Her husband had been dishonorably discharged from the Army, making him ineligible for benefits or support services, and he was subsequently incarcerated. Even when her husband was in the service, they had to apply for food stamps to make ends meet.
>
> When they were referred to Homeward Deployed, Melissa and her toddler were about to be evicted. Because of HIPPA laws, Melissa was given Homeward Deployed's contact information but their staff could not be given her contact information. Multiple attempts were made through the referring agency to encourage Melissa to call. Like many people in her situation, she was never able to make the call and ask for support.
>
> Had her husband been honorably discharged, he could have transferred his GI Bill benefits to Melissa and she could have pursued workforce training so that she could find a good job and support their child on her own. Now, she is on her way to a family shelter where she will depend on the resources of her community to find a way to create a good life for herself and her child.

America's Guard and Reserve are 66% Army, 21% Air Force, 7% Navy, 5% Marine Corps, and 1% Coast Guard. The two Guard components, Army and Air Force, comprise 55% of this force; the Army National Guard has 362,000 members and the Air National Guard has 108,000.

Both the Guard and Reserve augment the active duty forces as necessary. The five Reserve branches work under the authority of the Department of Defense and report to the President as commander-in-chief. The Guard works under the authority of each State or territory and reports to the Governor as commander-in-chief, unless called to national service by the President. The National Guard Bureau provides policy, guidance, and support to the 54 States and Territories. Unfortunately, because each Guard state is essentially its own "franchise," the transition system for Guard is even more fragmented than it is for active duty Service Members.

	Total	Enlisted	Officer
Rank	850K+	85%	15%
Women	18%	18%	18%
Minorities	20%	88%	12%
Have HS Diploma/GED or less	80%	92%	8%
Have BA or Higher	20%	16%	84%
Average Age	32	31	40
Under 25	33%	38%	4%
Under 30	52%	58%	16%
Living outside the U.S.	1%	n/a	n/a

After two years of efforts, fewer than a third of Guard states use the National Guard Bureau's Employment Network. The network provides resume writing, interview skills training, a jobs database, and an industry gold-standard case management system to provide outcomes data. Some states have their own system, other states have no system. In some states, a "system" is just one person responsible for employment transition for every Guard soldier in their state.

To make matters worse, the DoD launched their own Hero2Hired portal and rebuffed attempts by the National Guard Bureau to collaborate and coordinate. Employers now have to connect individually with employment staff from every Guard state, instead of using the centralized portal provided by the Guard Bureau, as well as with Hero2Hired. In addition, they are being heavily courted by the U.S. Chamber of Commerce to participate in its Hiring Our Heroes job fairs. This creates tremendous confusion and complication for even the most dedicated Veteran-friendly companies.

While the National Guard has always supplemented the fighting forces of the Active duty military, Guard members have traditionally responded to protect life and property on U.S. soil, often after natural disasters like Hurricane Sandy. Over the past 20 years, the National Guard has seen the nature of its Federal mission change, most dramatically with hundreds of thousands of Guard members serving in Iraq and Afghanistan since the September 11 attacks, many in repeat deployments.

Members of the National Guard and Reserve are typically older, many having left active duty and transitioned into the Guard or Reserve to continue a tradition of Service. This is especially true of Guard and Reserve officers. They are more likely to be married and have children. They work full-time and spend one weekend a month and two weeks every summer drilling and receiving military training.

Many Guard members enlist because drill pay supplements their income. A new Guard E1 will earn roughly $3,000 a year in drill pay. A Guard officer with 20+ years of experience may earn more than $20,000 a year in drill pay. Many post-9/11 Guard enlisted when a deployment was announced, or volunteered to deploy when they lost their jobs as a way to provide stable income for their families. Guard members earn pay using the active duty pay scale equivalent to their Guard rank when deployed.

"Ray" lost his job as a yacht painter in a rural community in 2009. He enlisted in the National Guard in order to take care of his family. Let that sink in a minute. An unemployed boat painter volunteered to go to combat as his best strategy to feed his family. When I met Ray at a demobilization event, I strongly suspected he had undiagnosed PTSD and I knew he would be unlikely to receive treatment back home in his rural community. So, Ray still had no job and potentially had PTSD complicating his transition home and search for employment.

Ray's parents encouraged him to get his commercial driver's license and become a long-haul trucker like his daddy. The transition folks encouraged this; they needed to show they had Ray on a transition pathway. But, Ray had a wife and three little girls under the age of 10. He had just been away for 15 months. He didn't want to be away 27 days a month driving trucks cross country. Like most men, he wanted to be with his wife and see his little girls grow up. Who would help Ray find a job when he returned home? Who would support his wife in dealing with Ray's apparent mental health issues? How would his three little girls be impacted by all of this? Thousands of men like Ray are already at home, struggling to find a way ahead. Main Street is the only safety net Ray and his family have.

The frequency of Guard deployments post-9/11 has created serious unemployment problems for Guard members. Prior to 9/11, Guard were rarely if ever deployed abroad and most employers were willing to comply with Federal regulations requiring them to give employees who were members of the Guard two weeks a year of unpaid leave for summer drill. However, the frequency and duration of Guard deployments post-9/11 have created unemployment rates nationwide of 34% for our Guard, with some Guard units demobilizing from deployment showing a 68% unemployment rate.

Federal Uniformed Services Employment and Reemployment Rights Act (USERRA) laws designed to protect Service Members' jobs, like so many laws, have proven difficult to enforce. Understandably given the recent decade of multiple Guard deployments, civilian employers are increasingly hesitant to hire Guard and Reserve. The negative impact on workflow and business revenue from repeat deployments is significant, especially for small businesses in the current economic environment. Sadly, our Federal agencies are some of the worst offenders of USERRA law violations.

Compounding the problem of Guard unemployment is the military-civilian divide. In Congressional testimony, Guard leadership essentially pointed the finger at civilian employers, suggesting that they are unpatriotic and calling for businesses to adapt to Guard deployment schedules. Employers responded that they could not continue to lose millions of dollars attributed to Guard deployments, jeopardizing their financial stability in an unpredictable and increasingly competitive global economy. If this pattern continues, the predictable future is that our National Guard will continue to experience high rates of unemployment.

When Guard and Reserve reintegrate home following return from deployment, they often have no transition or decompression time. The Guard's Yellow Ribbon Reintegration weekends are not any more effective than the active duty Service's Transition Assistance Program. The Guard and Reserve by nature are geographically dispersed. Soldiers may live hundreds of miles from the nearest armory so access to services can be difficult if not impossible.

> "Cindy" dutifully participated in a Yellow Ribbon event after she got back from deployment, feeling an obligation to set an example as an officer. She describes the event as being fire-hosed with information, most of it useless. Having been deployed three times now, she laughs and shows me a file box full of brochures and fact sheets that she never read.

Guard/Reserve families cannot get the support from their military community that active duty families get by virtue of living on or near a military installation. Active duty military families have large support systems from their peers since military units deploy or demobilize as a group. Since Guard and Reserve families are not as mobile, spouses often live and work in civilian communities where they experience tremendous isolation.

> Hugo, Minnesota, holds monthly hamburger dinners at the American Legion to raise money for direct assistance to Guard families. The dinners also provide a sense of community and show public appreciation for Guard families during and after deployment. Attendance has increased 400% in 18 months and in August 2012 Hugo had 170 people in attendance. There is a six month waiting list to be the community business sponsor of the hamburger dinner. Efforts like these make a huge difference in the lives of Guard/Reserve families and also strengthen Hugo's sense of community.

The children of Guard members attend predominantly civilian schools where teachers and staff may lack awareness of the impact of military service on children's well-being. And, like their parents, Guard children typically lack the peer support that their active duty counterparts enjoy.

> The Minnesota Yellow Ribbon communities have piloted a curriculum, now available state-wide, to bridge the military-civilian divide in their public schools. Civilian peers learn about their military counterparts. Now, when military kids say, "My dad just deployed," their friends know not to speculate about if he'll come home or how many people he might kill. They can be better friends and part of a support network for their peers. And, everyone has learned valuable lessons in compassion, empathy, and teamwork. Isn't that what schools and parents want for their students?

Roughly 130,000 Guard and Reserve leave the service each year (10% officers and 90% enlisted). It is not clear how the drawdown will impact the Guard and Reserve. Some DOD insiders have predicted a massive drawdown within the Guard as the country ends two wars. However, in August 2012, Defense Secretary Leon Panetta affirmed the importance of the Guard to national defense strategy, so that mission may not change with the end of the wars and the draw-down. Essentially, unlike our active duty forces, the National Guard can be rapidly scaled up or down to meet changing DoD needs in military N-strength.

These factors are wreaking havoc on the lives of Guard and Reserve members as well as their families. It is not uncommon for a member of the Guard or Reserve to be called up for deployment, quit or take leave from a job, and report to a military installation for training, only to have their deployment cancelled. This leaves Guard and Reserve members without the deployment pay they counted on and unemployed back home on Main Street. It is not unheard of for Guard units in these situations to face 70% unemployment.

Hurricane Sandy was a brutal reminder that these factors threaten the security of Main Street. The primary mission of the National Guard is to protect civilian lives and property in the aftermath of natural or human disasters, not to deploy overseas to combat missions. After Sandy, many communities relied on their National Guard for weeks for housing and food disbursements as well as physical security. With the instability deployments cause Guard members and their families, the Guard may face recruiting barriers in the future. If the Guard cannot attract quality members, our lives and the lives of those we love, our homes, and our workplaces may be put at risk. Just food for thought.

LGBT Service Members

The issues impacting our Lesbian, Gay, Bisexual, and Transgender Service Members are particularly complex given the divisiveness of this issue in American culture. With the repeal of Don't Ask, Don't Tell (DADT) in December 2010, and full implementation in September 2011, America's active duty Service Members could reveal their true identity. This has brought some measure of normalcy and dignity to our LGBT Service Members, who no longer have to hide their spouses and partners or deflect questions about their personal lives.

Steve was a member of the National Guard and a combat Veteran. Under Don't Ask, Don't Tell, he was afraid that the military would find out that he was gay and throw him out. Steve and his husband, Sam, lived in another state so that there would be almost no chance that someone would bump into them at the grocery store, out to dinner, or at the movies.

When Steve developed severe PTSD after returning from combat, he was afraid to go to the VA for help because the financial disclosure forms would have revealed that all of his assets—his home, cars, and investment portfolio—were also in Sam's name. Fortunately, Steve was connected with Give an Hour where he could receive confidential support. Sam received no formal support and was left struggling to figure things out by himself. Fortunately, Steve and Sam are thriving again, but many like them are not.

Our LGBT military families are denied the basic access to services that their heterosexual counterparts enjoy because the Defense of Marriage Act (DOMA) precludes the DOD from recognizing these marriages and thus providing benefits. For example, a gay Service Member cannot have his or her spouse live with them on base. Their spouses cannot get base passes, health insurance, or access to the commissary or exchange. The children in these families may be denied health care and access to high quality military child care facilities until legal adoptions can be completed after they are born, adoptions that are not available to gay couples in many states. These families cannot join Family Readiness Groups or access support systems during deployments.

Ashley Broadway is legally married to Lt. Colonel Heather Mack; they have been together for 15 years and have two children. The only way Ashley could receive a base pass at Fort Bragg was by being classified as the care-giver to their children. In a widely publicized case, Ashley applied to join the Fort Bragg Officer's Spouse Club and was turned away because she did not have a Fort Bragg spouse identification card. With overwhelming support, she was named Fort Bragg's "Military Spouse of the Year." And, she was offered a full membership in the Officer's Spouse Club.

These families are also often denied basic compassion. There have been instances where gay spouses and partners were denied base access to visit a seriously wounded spouse or partner. Gay spouses and partners are not eligible for recognition at the funerals of their loved ones or formal support services to help them move forward with life. Fortunately, Tragedy Assistance Program for Survivors (TAPS) is available to help these families.

> Tracy and Donna Johnson were legally married in the District of Columbia; both serve in the military. When Donna was killed in combat, Tracy was not formally notified by the military. She was denied the health care benefits, tuition assistance, and $1,200 monthly payment she would have received if she had been married to a male soldier. Heartbreakingly, NBC reported that when Tracy escorted Donna's body home from Dover Air Force Base, she was asked to carry Donna's wedding ring....which Federal policy dictated must be given to Donna's mother. Donna's mother promptly gave it back to Tracy. With no entitlements to bereavement support, Tracy will rely on organizations like TAPS and other support systems on Main Street as she adjusts to life as a young widow.

A significant fear that military leadership associated with the lifting of DADT was that it would adversely affect unit cohesion, especially among deployed troops. Given that the majority of combat troops are under 30, and this demographic has very different views on homosexuality, it is not surprising that these fears have proven completely unfounded. Instead, we see a very subtle emerging trend. Unit cohesion is being affected because straight Service Members are becoming increasingly uncomfortable as they realize the disparity in entitlements between their families and the families of their gay counterparts.

The purpose of this book is to help you understand what is happening with our post-9/11 military. I am not asking you to approve of gay marriage. I am not asking you to like gay people. But, I do feel compelled to leave you with a question on this issue. Are you comfortable, as an American citizen, asking young men and women to put their lives at risk and potentially die defending you, your country, and the ideals of democracy....only to tell them that when they return home, they cannot pursue the loving relationships that will help them heal and transition? Is this really what democracy means to you? Just more food for thought.

MILITARY SPOUSES AND PARTNERS

ACTIVE DUTY	Total	Enlisted	Officer
Average Age	31	30	36
Spouse Under 30	55%	61%	27%
Spouse not in the workforce	39%	37%	45%
Spouse Unemployment	12%	16%	9%
Married	56%	54%	70%
Married, Dual Military	7%	6%	1%
Active duty Parents	44%	9%	35%
Married w/ Kids	39%	n/a	n/a
Married w/Kids, Dual Military	2.9%	n/a	n/a
Single Parent	5%	n/a	n/a

GUARD AND RESERVE	Total	Enlisted	Officer
Average Age	36	35	40
Spouse Under 30	33%	38%	13%
Spouse not in the workforce	n/a	n/a	n/a
Spouse Unemployment	n/a	n/a	n/a
Married	48%	44%	71%
Married, Dual Military	3%	2%	<1%
Parents	43%	40%	59%
Married w/ Kids	9%	n/a	n/a
Married w/Kids, Dual Military	1.4%	n/a	n/a
Single Parent	9%	n/a	n/a

America's active duty Service Members bring with them about 2 million immediate family members, roughly 800,000 spouses and 1.2 million children. Our Guard and Reserve have around 1.2 million immediate family members, roughly 413,000 spouses and 746,000 children. These numbers do not reflect unmarried partners and their children, who could easily comprise another 1 million people or more.

Given that the military is almost 90% male, military spouses and partners are typically female. They are offered services through their closest military installation, often in the form of family readiness groups (known as FRGs) or pastoral care. However, for spouses or partners who live off base, especially our National Guard and Reserve spouses, these services are often not accessible. During a spouse or partner's deployment, it is common for these spouses to move home to be near family, often making services virtually inaccessible. Unmarried military partners are not eligible for any services, and may not even be able to enter the local base.

While the military has been reasonably progressive in its policies toward female Service Members, attitudes towards spouses remain Victorian at best. Military spouses and partners are expected to subsume their careers for their spouse's. Women, especially the wives of officers, are expected to take on enormous unpaid duties simply because they are wives....running the local FRG, assisting the families of the wounded and the fallen, hosting official dinners, etc. A Service Member whose spouse does not comply with expectations may find it difficult to get promoted. This puts significant strains on military marriages as well as on military spouses who want to pursue a career and/or raise children. "Darlene" shared the following story about being an officer's wife and Family Readiness Group leader:

> "My husband was deployed and I was the FRG leader for about 500 families. I got a call that one of the young moms, whose husband was deployed with my husband, had just had a stillborn child. I had to find a sitter for my own three kids, who were all under ten.

I rushed to the hospital, the mom was hysterical and they were about to sedate her. They handed me this dead baby. Meanwhile, the doctor had her husband on the phone telling him that he needed to come home from South Korea to be with her. But, he was about to separate from the service and planned to stay in South Korea with his Korean girlfriend. He was refusing to come home to take care of his wife. Then, they handed the phone to me to try to reason with him.

So, there I was holding a dead baby and yelling at this man about doing the right thing. It's not like I got training for this kind of stuff. It's not like I get paid for this, not even reimbursement for childcare. And, my own husband was deployed, so I didn't have support at home either."

Darlene was in some ways lucky to be an Army wife; she had a support system. Had Darlene been a Guard wife, she would have depended on her civilian neighbors and friends to be her support system. Offering support is a really simple way that we as civilians can support our military families.

Military culture is one of transience. Moving every two to three years, often cross-country or overseas, makes it difficult or even impossible for our military spouses to find and keep employment. Licenses and credentials often do not translate across state lines. Resumes can look "unstable" because of frequent moves. This contributes to a sad trend for our young military families who increasingly turn to food stamps and other public assistance programs in order to make ends meet. In response to military culture coupled with frequent moves and repeat cycles of deployment, roughly a third of military spouses are not a part of the workforce, putting them and their children at serious economic disadvantage should they divorce.

Tamara is a lawyer. At 30, she married an Army officer. After their first Permanent Change of Station (PCS), Tamara studied for the bar in her new state of residence; she had to pay out-of-pocket for the study courses and the cost of retaking the bar. It took her almost a year. When their next PCS took them to a state that did not have reciprocity for either state in which she had passed the bar, she gave up and volunteered her legal services at local nonprofits. Now that her husband has been promoted to Colonel, she is expected to run the FRG, organize fundraisers, visit the families of the fallen and wounded, and host and attend social events. All for no pay. She misses her legal career and resents being treated like a free resource to the Army; the stress, lack of fulfillment, and resentment is beginning to seep into her marriage. Tamara would be well served by her country if the dialogue around standardized credentialing would move forward faster.

The number of repeat deployments has contributed to a record-setting 30,000 military marriages ending in divorce in 2011, with divorce rates among the services ranging from 3.7% to 5% compared to 3.7% for the civilian population. The divorce rate is two to three times higher for female Service Members. This may be in part because most male Service Members marry civilians while most female Service Members marry other Service Members. Sadly, no one counts divorce among our post-9/11 Veteran population but some people place that number as high as 70% within two years of return from deployment.

Finally, domestic abuse in military families has increased by 30% since 2006. Coupled with the rise in civilian domestic abuse resulting from the current economic downturn, local domestic abuse hotlines, counseling programs, and shelters are working in constant overwhelm and running out of money before the end of their fiscal years. Clients may wait weeks and sometimes months for services. As a result, women and children of all walks of life, including our military families, are suffering unnecessary physical injuries and mental scarring compounded by limited or no access to services to help them heal and move forward. This often starts or reinforces generational cycles of poverty, homelessness, substance abuse, mental health issues, and child maltreatment for these women and their children.

Terrence and Jackie had been high school sweethearts. They married right out of high school and Terrence enlisted in the Army. After his first deployment, he pulled a loaded shotgun on Jackie. When he was home during his mid-tour R&R, while Jackie was pregnant with their second child, he tried to strangle her to death. She calls it "the incident." Terrence cut Jackie off from his benefits when she left him. He convinced his commanding officer that she was preventing him from seeing his children. His tricks were illegal but eventually Jackie got tired of trying to fight the system and divorced him, giving up benefits and access to support services in the process.

She and her two young children moved in with her mom and step-dad. Jackie is working on her associate degree and she did an internship with a Fortune 50 company. She has a plan to get her bachelor degree and would eventually like to start a business. But, her step-dad is tired of the noise and commotion. He wants her and her kids out. Now she needs a job, safe low-cost housing, and quality child-care. Jackie has a lot of potential, but she's going to need some help to get there. And, if she gets the help she needs on Main Street, everyone wins.

The National Military Family Association does great work with policy and advocacy for America's military families but they do not provide direct services beyond scholarships for military spouses to attend school and Camp Purple for military children. Many employers are expanding their Veteran programs to include military spouses. There is really no single go-to organization for spouses and partners, although many small organizations exist and hundreds of blogs offer advice and support. "Her War, Her Voice," a personal favorite, is a virtual forum for active duty military wives and a great place to learn about what military spouses go through.

Military Children

There are roughly 2 million military children, 1.3 million of whom are under the age of 11. America's young military children have spent their entire lives with one or both parents at war. Think about the infants, toddlers, and elementary school children in your life. Now imagine what their lives would be like if they had never known a time when they were not impacted by deployment or worried about the death of a parent in combat. Never, not for a single day. Imagine a life where daddy or mommy, or both, are in war zones more than they are home celebrating birthdays and watching soccer games. Stop and let that sink in for a moment.

	Active	Reserve
Total Number	1.2M	746K
Birth to 5	42%	28%
6 to 11	31%	30%
12 to 18	23%	30%
19 to 22	4%	12%

Over the coming decade, we may see our population of post-9/11 military children grow to 4 or 5 million as their parents settle down and start or grow their families. What happens from birth to five, when a child's brain develops rapidly, determines the extent to which that child will have what they need to succeed in school and in life. Recent research suggests that the single biggest risk factor on the brain development of young children is living in a household with persistent stress and/or inconsistent parenting.

A friend of mine teaches baby care and Lamaze at a military hospital. She worked with a pregnant Service Member who was scheduled to be deployed to South Korea when her baby was six weeks old. Her husband was in the Service and the military would not coordinate their duty stations so that they could stay stateside or deploy together. The mom could not take her baby to Korea as a single parent. So, the baby would be left in the care of his dad, who was 21 and had never changed a diaper.

Yes, this couple knew before conceiving a child that this was a possibility. But, let me ask you a question. Is it reasonable for young military couples to have to forego parenthood because they serve in the military? Can you recognize the serious risk to this infant, being raised by a young dad who has never cared for a baby? Can you see the risk to the mom for serious post-partum depression? Can't you imagine that in the 21st century the DoD might be able to find a compassionate, responsible way for its employees to balance Duty to Country and Duty to Family?

Maternal stress and depression—which affect 11% of mothers with non-deployed spouses, 27% of mothers with deployed spouses, and 68% of spouses caring for wounded warriors—is the single largest risk factor for the healthy development of these young children. At any given time, roughly a quarter of our young military children, nearly 200,000, are being cared for by a stressed or depressed mother. And, my guess would be that many of the 1.3 million children from birth to 11 have spent a significant part of their lives in high stress families. Not because they have bad parents but because their parents are not getting the deployment and transition support they need to manage their stress effectively so that they can parent well. This sets the stage for cycles of difficulty and failure as these children enter their school years and eventually transition into adulthood.

About 20% of military preschoolers exhibit troubling behaviors, such as hitting, biting, and tantruming, twice the rate for their civilian peers. Nearly a third of military elementary school children are considered at "high risk" for inability to function normally in social groups, 2.5 times the rate of their civilian peers.

> Most of the children at Fort Belvoir Elementary School, on post at Fort Belvoir but part of Fairfax County Public Schools, have had one or both parents at war their entire lives. Virtually all of the children, including the small percentage from a nearby low-income housing, have lost a parent or know a student who has lost a parent. Fort Belvoir ES has had third graders put into in-patient psychiatric care for secondary post-traumatic stress. The amount of stress on these families is so intense that a local organization provided the money to place two full-time psychologists on-site to work

with the students and families. The staff cleared out space and furnished offices. Sadly, placement of these much-needed support staff was delayed by months due to red-tape and paperwork, harming families in the process. Creating an expedited process for positive supports for military families is one way schools can support their military students.

While the children of our active duty Service Members often have peer groups, our Guard and Reserve children often find themselves isolated and unprepared to handle the stresses of the deployment cycle. On top of the social and emotional issues, because of the transience of military life, our military children are constantly changing schools. They are often repeating curricula or coursework because of differences in education standards between states. Middle and high school students are sometimes forced to repeat coursework because credits do not transfer across state lines or graduation requirements are different. America's Promise, founded by Colin and Alma Powell, has been active in mobilizing states to sign the Military Interstate Children's Compact; sadly, 20% of states still refuse to sign the Compact and the implementation has proven very slow in filtering down to the school district officials and principals who actually administer the Compact.

Often, it is the transition and reintegration period following return from deployment that is the hardest for America's military children and their families. The anxiety level of children actually rises from 23% to 32% upon a parent's return from deployment. Studies have shown that Service Members often have a higher level of stress during the family reintegration phase, largely attributed to the stress of helping their children cope.

Alarmingly, America's Promise has recently identified military children as "at risk" to not achieve productive adulthood alongside their peers who live in poverty, are members of minority groups, are recent immigrants, or have disabilities. They are working to engage their 400+ partner organizations to work together to find solutions to the challenges facing our military children, as well as all at-risk/at-promise youth.

Of course, not all families have poor family outcomes as a result of the reintegration period. A strong marriage and a good social support network contribute to family transition resilience; however, many of our Guard families transition in isolation without a good support network. Military families report that three things make transitioning easier: believing that their sacrifice made a difference, having a strong family, and believing that America supports the wars.

With more than 2 million post-9/11 military children, and likely another 2 or 3 million on the way over the next decade, it is critical for communities to find ways to support the healthy development of these children. These 4 or 5 million children will attend public school in Hometown America, thriving or disproportionately disrupting classrooms and taking teacher/staff time for remedial or support services. If these children fail to thrive, like all children who fail to thrive, they will disproportionately drop out of school, abuse substances, give birth to at-risk babies, become entangled in the criminal justice system, and become temporary or permanent burdens to their communities. If these children thrive, like all children who thrive, they will become productive adults, engaged citizens, and community leaders. It is in America's best interest to make sure these children, and all children, thrive.

POST-9/11 VETERANS

Much less research has been done on our post-9/11 Veterans, in part because they can be hard to find after they separate from the service. It is shocking but true that separating Service Members are not asked for their cell phone number or email address as they out-process!

As these Veterans transition out of the service, their spouses, partners, and children are transitioning with them. Many couples have delayed having children or expanding their family because of multiple deployments. This becomes a primary goal upon separation from the Service, compounding financial pressures and relationship stress. A young student Veteran reports:

> "Now that I'm home, my wife wants to have a baby. I want to use my GI Bill and get my degree. My GI Bill money won't cover living expenses for a family. I don't see how I can do well in school and work to support my wife and a baby. She just needs to wait four years until I'm done. Then, we can have a baby. She's really angry because she says she has already waited four years while I was constantly deploying. We fight about it all the time."
>
> If this young couple is lucky, they have a family who can help them sort this out. If not, they may need some support from community or campus services. Failure to get services will increase the likelihood that they will divorce, or that they will have a baby and he will end up dropping out of school. Everyone loses.

Many young Veterans have no family or community to turn to. So, as they separate from the Service, they leave the only family and support system they have ever known. Others move home to states with very high unemployment rates to be near family, or face giving up the support of family to move to a community where they can find a job. For many enlisted who joined the Service straight out of high school, they return to Main Street ill-prepared to find housing and doctors, write resumes and look for employment, apply to college, or manage their money.

It is a misperception that these Veterans have access to limitless benefits and support programs; the benefit structures are very complex and many young Veterans who serve just four years are entitled to relatively little support. The spouses and children of active duty Service Members receive limited services beyond healthcare and access to childcare. Available services for the spouses, partners, and children of Veterans are nearly nonexistent. This is especially true for our LGBT Veterans and their families.

Contrary to the popular hype, Veterans' military skills often do not translate easily or completely into the civilian workforce. Veterans who attended the voluntary Transition Assistance Program are often primed to believe that America is waiting to hire them, only to begin job hunting and find out that their skill sets are not competitive and employers don't understand their resumes. They find that they cannot recreate their military pay grade on Main Street, so they face taking jobs that significantly lower their quality of life.

> Someone forwarded a friend's resume to me. He was a Navy Veteran. I looked at his resume. How cool! He trained dolphins to detect mines on battleships. It would be a great basis for a made-for-TV movie but it wasn't going to get him very far in the civilian job market unless he was hoping to work at Sea World.
>
> I could see the skills and talents embedded in his resume, but I'm a coach who works with Veterans. The average civilian employer would smile and throw it in the circular file.
>
> When you run a small business, you often get more than 100 resumes every time you post a job. As the person hiring, you need to "get" the resume in the first 15 seconds. It's the applicant's job to effectively pitch you, not the other way around. This is not the message our transitioning military are getting as they separate from the Service, and it's hurting them. It sets them up for failure in a competitive job market. Employers, community chambers of

commerce, and retired Vietnam-era Veterans can provide meaningful help to these transitioning Veterans by volunteering resume help. When a post-9/11 Veterans transitions into a job, reducing his or her risk for transition failure, we all win.

Since 9/11, many military have re-enlisted to avoid the job market struggle on Main Street. Until recently, the military was delighted to have them re-enlist. However, with the end of the wars and beginning of the drawdown, many Veterans are finding themselves separating from the Service because they are not offered contract renewals. These numbers will significantly increase over the next five years as the pace of the drawdown accelerates. A Marine colonel put it to me this way:

> "Imagine that we have told this young guy or gal that they are a Marine for Life. We put them in combat three, four, five times. Maybe they have a disability or PTSD. With the drawdown, we shake their hands, thank them for their sacrifice, and show them the door. Now, they are home on Main Street and they are angry, they feel betrayed. Now imagine hundreds of thousands of Veterans like this on Main Street. Our communities are going to get hit with a tsunami and they don't even know it's coming."

Like their peers from other wars, many of America's post-9/11 Veterans face a loss of identity upon separating from the Service. In the Service, they were an 88mike or an 11bravo. They were defined by these military occupational specialties and their rank. They knew the rules of social engagement simply by reading rank, which everyone wears on their chest. Back home on Main Street, often with no experience as an adult establishing relationships outside military culture, they are at a disadvantage. They can feel and appear socially awkward simply because they are learning a new set of rules for social engagement, causing them to further isolate themselves and intensify transition stress.

I met a young Veteran at a local Chamber of Commerce networking event. He introduced himself as "Victor" and said he was looking for a job. Someone had suggested he go to Chamber mixers. I asked Victor what he did. He promptly replied, "I'm a sniper." I invited him to step into a quiet corner and helped him to re-invent his elevator speech. Now that Victor was out of the military, he was no longer a sniper. And, while I knew several businesses that were hiring, none were looking for snipers. Yes, he had attended his transition program. Sigh.

On top of this, America's post-9/11 Veterans face a challenge unique to their generation....the search for passion and purpose. Many of our Service Members enlisted in response to the attacks of September 11, 2001; they were driven by patriotism and a desire to defend America. Now that they are back home on Main Street, they are searching for an equally meaningful sense of purpose and mission, something that they can be as passionate about as they were about their military service. And, working at the local construction site or becoming an accountant is just not working for them.

Iraq and Afghanistan Veterans of America is a young organization that has proven very adept at policy and advocacy work, successfully advancing many Veteran-friendly bills into law. However, laws without funding have proven to be less than effective. Life "beyond the yellow ribbon," is akin to turning young post-9/11 Veterans loose into a football stadium full of vending machines, giving them a roll of quarters and hoping they pick the right machine to give them what they need to transition well.

Part of my purpose in writing this little book is to start a focused national dialogue about how to create a coordinated framework for post-9/11 Veteran transition. That is one of the reasons that I am launching Troops to Towns for city/county managers and other community leaders: to help them in creating this framework in their local community. And, in painting a big vision, it is my hope that there can be a warm handoff from Transition GPS to a Homeward Deployed coach, so that any Veteran in any community knows how to find a live person to help them get the services they need to transition.

It is not my goal to make Homeward Deployed or Troops to Towns the end-all, be-all for Veteran transition but a place to start, where Veterans can find a savvy, compassionate human conduit that connects them to the myriad fabulous organizations that can help them transition. What do you do when you land at the airport of a strange city? You check the information booth. Think of Troops to Towns as that information booth. What do you do when you check into a hotel? You talk to the concierge. Think of a Homeward Deployed coach as a transition concierge.

STUDENT VETERANS

On the surface of it, the GI Bill seems like a great pathway for our young Veterans to get the training, credentialing, and the degrees they need to put them on a stable pathway to economic self-sustain-ability. GI Bill money can be used at community colleges and four year degree granting institutions. It can also be used to attend technical training programs and apprenticeship programs in the trades.

More than 1 million post-9/11 Veterans have taken advantage of their GI Bill benefits. Tragically, these benefits are having anything but the anticipated outcomes. As many as 88% percent of Veterans are reported to drop out of school, although this number is being hot-ly contested by Student Veterans of America. The United States has spent more than $17 billion in GI Bill benefits; so, even if the number is closer to 50%, it is clear that huge sums of money have been wasted that could support transition services that are effective.

Research is just now getting underway to study the breakdown in the system. Meanwhile, as a person with a background in higher and adult education, I can suggest some explanations based on what I have seen which may guide us in supporting our Student Veterans to success.

First, Service Members are strongly encouraged to use their GI Bill benefits, regardless of whether college is a good fit for them. College never has, and never will be, the right place for everyone. Only 30% of the general population ever goes to college; why would it be different for Veterans? We start or reinforce cycles of failure by encouraging Veterans to go to college if it is not in fact a good fit for them.

> "Brian" is a disabled combat Veteran with a 100% disability rating. He has a moderate traumatic brain injury. He's smart and engaging. Everyone tells him that he should use his GI Bill and get a degree. No one listens when he tells them he has no short term memory. One day, he asked me, "How can I go to college when I can't remember worth shit?" Yes, there are accommodations but for Brian it really might not be a good fit. And, he already has great skills, if an employer could see past the fact that he only has a high school degree and walks with a cane.

Second, the message is, "Enroll in college and figure out what you want to do once you get there." This is a terrible idea! First, many student Veterans arrive on campus while they are still decompressing. They are not in an ideal place to manage the culture shock of transitioning from the highly structured environment of the military to the loose structure of a college campus. This is compounded by the fact that many if not most of America's post-9/11 Veterans arrive on campus with no clue why they are there. In their military service, they were clear about purpose and mission. Now, they find themselves ambling around looking for purpose and passion. They feel like they are drifting and they often perceive that they are "behind" compared to their younger peers. A student Veteran shares a classroom experience:

> "I deployed twice. I was an artillery guy in combat. I commanded a whole unit. I knew what I was doing. I was good at it. Now, I'm sitting here in Introduction Biology and we're going to dissect frogs. I'm thinking, what's the point? I should just go get a job, do something meaningful."

Third, we overlook the fact that Student Veterans are in fact a special category of older adult students. Older adult students often do not feel like they fit in with campus culture. They don't connect with younger classmates who spend weekends binge drinking and skipping classes. Like 75% of Student Veterans, they are juggling marriages, parenting, and jobs with school responsibilities. Like many older students, Veterans may have lost the study skills they had in high school. They may need remedial assistance in math and English. They are embarrassed to ask for help and the support systems to provide this assistance are inadequate. This is the typical experience of older, non-traditional college students. Coupled with simultaneous military transition, however, college campuses are labeled by Student Veterans as "unfriendly" or anti-Veteran. Remember the part about "you can never go home again?" A student Veteran shared this story:

> "I was sitting in a class in Middle East History and Politics. The professor was talking about the battle of Fallujah. I was actually there! Most of the kids in my class were in kindergarten riding around on their scooters. I was 27 but I felt so old and out of place."

Fourth, while many colleges and universities are scaling up their Veteran services on campus, many student Veterans just "want to be normal" and choose not to use the support services they desperately need to feel connected and purposeful on campus. Student Veterans of America is a great organization that was established to provide Veterans on campus with peer support but even they can have trouble connecting with their own members. At one local campus in Virginia, fewer than 50 of 1800 Student Veterans use the campus Veterans Center located in the student union.

> "Andy" complained, "I'm tired of being 'the Veteran.' I'm tired of people asking me if I killed people. I just want to be 'normal,' to fit in." Then, he gave me one of the compliments I most value and carry with me: "What

I like about you is that you don't see me as 'GI Joe.' You see me as a real person, an individual with unique needs."

Many Veterans who are at colleges or universities might be better served by being in technical training or apprenticeship programs. Many of the trades—automotive mechanics, plumbing, electrical, CAD/CAM machinists, utility linesmen, etc.—offer salaries above the national average for experienced workers and these professions will never be outsourced overseas. However, across the United States, we have lost the dignity of the trades and the stigma of a job where you "get your hands dirty" is a barrier to entry for young Veterans and civilians alike. Entry into the trades is further complicated by myriad scandals involving technical schools that lure Veterans into their programs for the sole purpose of getting their GI Bill money, with no thought or care to providing the support services these Veterans need to be successful.

Many excellent apprenticeship programs, like Helmets to Hardhats, are offered through unionized trade associations. Unfortunately, their graduates find it difficult to gain employment because non-union employers are afraid to hire them for fear that they are "plants" who are really there on union business to "salt" their factories and mobilize their employees to become a union shop. They are not, but the stigma is there. We would do well to help our Veteran apprentices learn how to have candid conversations with employers to dispel these fears. And, for our civilian employers to consider why a Veteran might have been in a program like Helmets to Hardhats to begin with.

Figures place Veteran graduation rates as low as 3%; again, this is a hotly contested number. But even if the number is 10% or 20%, for many post-9/11 Veterans the promise of education paid for by their GI Bill becomes another opportunity to start or reinforce a cycle of failure. As part of a comprehensive national Veteran transition network, we need to ensure that our young Veterans receive better transition support to ensure that they make decisions that really work for their lives, rather than trying to fit them into a generic off-the-shelf solution that does not help them realize their goals. We need to make sure that the timing of college or other post-secondary education aligns with other facets of life. This kind of transition systems creates a win for everyone.

WOUNDED WARRIORS

Perhaps you have visited the Vietnam Veterans Memorial in Washington, D.C. It is very sobering to see a wall 246 feet long and up to 10 feet tall with 58,195 names etched into its black basalt face. Now imagine that wall six times as long, stretching more than a quarter of a mile....or reaching six stories in height. Take a moment and picture that. Because that is the size of the wall needed to etch the names of America's post-9/11 Wounded Warriors onto a wall. And, if we were to add the names of those suffering the invisible wounds of war, using conservative statistics, that wall would be at least half a mile long or 12 stories high with more than 600,000 names. Sit with that a minute; it's a lot to digest. It's a big wall to scale.

More than 100,000 post-9/11 military have been seriously physically injured. More than 200,000 have been diagnosed with Traumatic Brain Injuries (TBI), the "signature wound" of these wars, a number that may double as new technology is able to diagnose mild TBI. Advances in medical technology allow us to save critically wounded Service Members who in previous wars would have died, but the future we offer the seriously injured is precarious at best. Many will need lifetime care-giving because their injuries, while profound, do not significantly affect their life expectancy and they are mostly very young.

The vast majority of the seriously injured merit disability ratings that give them access to VA benefits but many wait up to two years to get through the system to receive the rating that creates eligibility. And, actually getting services is another story. Many disabled Veterans do not live near a VA facility; it may take an entire day to travel to a VA facility for treatment. Veterans can wait weeks, or even months, for diagnostic testing and surgeries. Beds for inpatient care are limited, which can also delay access to services.

> "I knew the minute I saw 'Danny' walk off the plane that he was not the same person," recounted a military mom. "At first, it wasn't too bad but then he started drinking. He broke up with his girlfriend. He would stay out all night. He started talking about killing himself, he told us he was a murderer.
>
> We finally got him into a VA clinic. They told us that he was a real risk for suicide but that they only had 12 beds. They gave us a card, told us to call every day to see if a bed opened up, and to watch him carefully. Danny hanged himself in our basement three days later."
>
> Increasingly, we are going to see families like Danny's looking for services on Main Street because they give up on the VA. Families like Danny's will need support as they move through the grieving process: neighbors who reach out, employers who can give extra time off, friends who make extra time for coffee or lunch.

VA facilities have a terrible reputation for the quality of outpatient care. Veterans consistently complain that they are simply given "bags of pills" and sent home, rather than developing a comprehensive recovery and wellness plan. And, the transition process for a wounded warrior extends beyond medical treatments. Many seriously injured need adaptive technologies, modifications to their homes, and special vehicles to live effectively as disabled people. Many will need rehabilitative services for a lifetime, just to maintain a baseline level of functioning.

> I was surprised to get a referral from the Wounded Warrior Project. They were working with a young Veteran with a serious TBI and a 100% disability rating. He was living at home with his parents in a rural community. His mom had quit her job to take care of him. He was working with an occupa-

tional therapist but the VA decided he was not making adequate progress and they terminated services. The Wounded Warrior Project wondered if we could provide a coach for him.

His needs went WELL beyond what coaches are trained to do. But, I was not going to be another part of the system that told this mom she would have to go it alone. So, I talked to a colleague who runs a local brain injury service. She agreed that she would provide one of her therapists to mentor a coach in the young man's community, to help the coach work with him. It was a truly inadequate plan but the alternative was no plan at all. I have to confess I was relieved that they never called for services.

As more of our seriously wounded transition home, we are going to see a real increase in the need for medical and psychological care from civilian systems that are currently unfamiliar with combat injuries. The people in these systems will need free and low-cost training to support these Veterans in leading productive lives.

And, then, there is the psychological care and transition process. Our Wounded Warriors must come to terms with the fact that the life they had before their injury is gone forever. They must come to accept and adapt to their new normal. This process is unique to every individual. While military leadership has embraced a more open culture around mental health issues, that has not filtered down to the actual staff running many Wounded Warrior regiments. I have heard horrifying stories of what amounts to boot camp-like abusive behavior directed at the severely wounded trying to cope with PTSD and not able to meet demands to be dressed, shaved, and ready for roll call at 0800.

There are stories of amputees, even multiple amputees, who transition seemingly effortlessly into life with prosthetics. And, there are stories of Wounded Warriors who are medically retired from the Service nowhere near ready to manage basic life functions on their own. Because the military is a highly structured environment, there is no room for individual timetables for recovery.

Many Wounded Warriors assume that their Service will find a place for them, only to realize weeks before medical discharge that they will not be returning to active duty. As a result, many seriously injured Veterans find themselves without access to desperately needed services when they are most vulnerable. And, after medical retirement, they face the same loss of identity as non-disabled Veterans but with the additional burden of simultaneously adjusting to life as a person with a disability.

> I have friends, "Charlie" and "Sue." Charlie was blown up by an IED and when he arrived from Landstuhl, they weren't sure he would ever work again. He went through 14 surgeries in two years. Sue quit her job so that she could be with him. I knew Charlie had turned the corner in his recovery when he joked about his injury, referring to it as a "Forrest Gump" injury.... he had 40% of his butt blown off. Everyone laughed but we knew it wasn't really funny.
>
> Sue told me that the worst part about her husband's combat injury and recovery was being medically retired from the Army. All of a sudden, they were on their own and they didn't know what to do. These amazingly resilient people actually fell apart. They're doing great now but we need to remember that transition and healing is often a lifetime journey that involves the mental and emotional as much as the physical. It is the family, friends, and neighbors on Main Street who will walk that pathway with our Wounded Warrior families.

The Fortune 500 and Wall Street have launched dozens of Wounded Warrior hiring programs, but their placement rate is dismal at best. Northrup Grummon's Operation Impact announced its 100th hire last year. The program has been operational for eight years and in 2011 Northrup Grummon boasted $26.4 billion in revenue, mostly in war dollars, from the efforts of 70,000 employees. The program's "Network of Champions" consists of more than 100 organizations, including many Fortune 500 companies; in 2010, they placed 12 Wounded

Warriors. That is not a typo: 12. I truly hate to point fingers but this is not a strategy that is going to help more than 300,000 seriously wounded Veterans and their families achieve fulfilling lives. These companies have made tens of billions of dollars from our wars in the Middle East; it is time for them to give back to help Veterans. The leaders on Main Street may have to do some nudging to get them to open their wallets.

Despite all of our efforts, many seriously injured will never again work in a traditional sense. However, properly supported, many of them can still be good spouses, parents, and community volunteers or leaders. Necessity is indeed the mother of invention. Anyone who has ever worked with a person with a disability knows that they are often very resourceful and creative because of the barriers they must overcome on a daily basis. As a nation, we cannot afford to discard potentially valuable community resources by failing to empower our Wounded Warriors in transition.

The Wounded Warrior Project provides exceptional life cycle support to Wounded Warriors, meeting them bedside in the trauma hospital in Landstuhl, Germany, and supporting them through the rest of their lives with peer mentoring, recreational opportunities, health and wellness services, workforce training, and employment transition support. However, these services cannot meet all the needs of more than 300,000 Wounded Warriors, especially as they move home and become geographically dispersed. These Veterans and their families will truly need a community of care as they transition home to Main Street.

WOUNDED WARRIORS CARE-GIVERS

For any seriously ill or injured person, the care-giver system is an anchor. Studies have shown that seriously ill or injured people transition twice as fast when they have a good support system. This is especially true for our Wounded Warriors who are often simultaneously rehabilitating while coping with combat trauma, isolation from their military community, and loss of identity not just as a whole healthy person but as an 88mike or 11 bravo. When a Wounded Warrior's care-giver system breaks down, they are at increased risk for never achieving the fullest possible recovery as well as for developing serious mental health issues or committing suicide. So, who anchors these care-givers? The answer is often no one.

> A colleague of mine who is a Marine Veteran went to visit his mother in a nursing home. When one of the nurses realized he was a Marine, she asked if he would stop in down the hall where a Marine wife was watching over her husband.
>
> Dan found a woman about 20 years old sitting quietly holding the hand of a young Marine. Dan learned that he had no cognitive functioning and would never recover beyond his present state. Neither of them had family. They had been "lost" in the Marine Corps system after he was moved to a civilian care facility. The wife was living in a low-rent motel and had been eating junk food from the nearby gas station with what little money she had left over after paying her hotel bill. When the nursing home discovered this, they began letting her eat with the residents at the nursing home.
>
> Without family, who was there to counsel this young woman? Our young Marine would never go with his wife to the movies, father children, or any of the things a normal young couple could look forward to. Who would help her grieve and let go, so that she could give herself permission to have a normal life? Because the only thing sadder than losing this young man, who now had no future, would be to lose both of them. Who would help her? Until Dan found her, the answer was, "No one."

America's young Wounded Warrior Care-givers are truly a forgotten group of people. With more than 300,000 seriously injured Service Members come at least 300,000 people in their care-giver networks. Many of the VA services as well as outreach to care-givers at the local/county level are geared towards older women caring for elderly men, with a heavy emphasis on Alzheimer's care. This is, of course, important for those care-givers. However, it offers nothing to a 24 year old young wife and mother who suddenly finds herself caring for her disabled husband, raising children, and perhaps becoming the sole bread-winner for her family as well.

The daily lives of many of these care-givers, like all care-givers providing family care, is physically and mentally exhausting. Schedules revolve around trips to the VA, surgeries, rehabilitation appointments, and counseling sessions. Endless hours are wasted waiting for appointment times that are not honored or struggling to find someone who can negotiate the complicated, antiquated VA benefits system which has yet to be fully digitized. Care-giver stress, for both military families and civilians, can cause serious illness and mental health issues for these care-givers. Kristle Helmuth is a young wounded warrior care-giver. She writes a blog called "The Story of Our Before and After." Here is one of her descriptions of care-giving:

> "We had a rough month last month. It was a month full of apathy and disinterest. This rough month that started in March is continuing into April and culminated tonight in a question that I often wonder, but always feel a bit guilty for thinking about. Who takes care of us? While there is more information out there about PTSD than ever before, there is surprisingly little about who takes care of the caregiver....it's all geared toward helping me help him.
>
> So, I ask you this, have you ever heard of secondary PTSD? I think of it as whiplash. I fly backwards in response to his outbursts and escalations and when I whip back forward, BAM a PTSD reaction to a situation full of heightened stress, fear, and emotion. And I completely understand why it's happening and can see where this will soon become the new normal for all of us. No one is taking care of us, while we take care of them.
>
> So, while my life is a battlefield full of land mines that are so expertly hidden that I have yet to learn to navigate the field. While my world is so full of fear and anxiety and stress that I can't sleep.... While I am carrying

this terrible burden and secret of our life, behind the passing glances of those who might peek into our windows... Who is going to be there when I am the one in need?

Increasingly we are hearing stories of care-giving families who are losing their homes to foreclosure because a family member must quit a job to take care of a Wounded Warrior. Retirement savings and home equities are rapidly depleted paying for expensive care outside the VA system by parents of Wounded Warriors who cannot get benefits eligibility quickly enough or who are disheartened at the poor quality of care available. This is, of course, true of many civilian care-givers, too, but our military care-givers are taking care of young men and women our nation chose to put in harm's way. I like to think that America has a responsibility to all disabled people, but it seems to me this is particularly true for people whose injuries occurred in large part due to the deliberate choices made by politicians we freely elect.

The Wounded Warrior Project offers retreats for care-givers and support in setting up community-based care-giver support systems. Having been a care-giver myself, a weekend away is a welcome breather but it can be the other 361 days a year that are the problem. Getting assistance with meals, carpools, and errands is wonderful. But, what many care-givers need is ongoing support to deal with overwhelm, grief, life-work balance, stress management, isolation, hopelessness, and the cycles of resentment and guilt that often accompany care-giving. And, often, care-givers, especially young care-givers, are so overwhelmed they cannot even reach out for the support they so desperately need; many of these young, vulnerable care-givers and their children are at serious risk for failure to thrive back home.

The Caregivers and Veterans Omnibus Health Services Act of 2010 was an important first step in providing assistance and support services for post-9/11 care-givers. It includes provisions for stipends, medical care, counseling, respite care, and travel costs for these care-givers. However, the funding set for these programs totals $500 million a year from 2011 to 2015. With more than 300,000 seriously injured and ill, that amounts to just $138 per month per family. And, with the case backlogs at the VA, it is likely that these families, like all Veterans, are waiting extended periods of time just to achieve eligibility.

If America does not want to lose our more than 300,000 seriously injured and ill post-9/11 Veterans, we must strengthen their most important recovery and support system....their family care-giver networks. This not only improves the quality of life for our Wounded Warriors and their care-givers, in the long term it reduces the burden of care falling on the communities who must support these young families as they return home to Main Street.

FAMILIES OF THE FALLEN AND THOSE WHO DIE BY SUICIDE

America has lost more than 6500 post-9/11 Service Members in theater and countless others to suicide related to Post-Traumatic Stress. Roughly 75% of military suicides are under 30 and enlisted; 72% served in the Army and 22% in the Marine Corps. Their spouses and partners, nearly all women, are likewise young and many leave young children behind.

When an Active duty Service Member is killed or commits suicide, their family quickly loses base housing. So, on top of grieving their loss, they also lose their homes and their communities of support. While other military spouses will initially rally around them, it is common for these friends to pull away....not because they are disloyal but because these military spouses and partners know that any day it could be them greeting Casualty Assistance Officers at their front door. Emotionally, it is often too wrenching to support a friend through the death of a spouse while keeping your own fears for your spouse in check.

Tragedy Assistance Program for Survivors provides exceptional services to these vulnerable families. They offer peer support networks, Good Grief camps, and retreats for military widows. They have recently begun the very important work of reaching out to the surviving families of suicide victims. Like our military care-giver population, these young women are often so overwhelmed that it is difficult for them to reach out for support, especially those who have lost a spouse or partner to suicide.

Many post-9/11 military widows lack the education and work experience to suddenly support their family. While these families do receive a $400,000 death benefit, that money will not support a family forever. And, there is no death benefit for suicide. So, often, these young women must re-enter the workforce or go back to school in isolation from their military support system while simultaneously grieving and raising children. Some of these young women have strong family support systems, but many do not.

> Carolina lost her husband, Carlos, less than a year ago. She is 35 and has two children, five and seven. She left her job to take care of Carlos following a combat injury and cancer diagnosis. As a single mom, she is afraid to go back to work as a detention officer because of the physical danger. She also knows it would be very difficult to find quality care for her two young children overnight and on weekends or holidays. She is fighting the VA for benefits, has no health insurance, and worries about getting sick. She was able to get health insurance and social security benefits for her children, but she feels guilty about using the money to pay for bills rather than putting it into their college fund.

> Carolina is worried about how she will find a stable job with a high school diploma and limited work experience. She is committed to being a good mother to her children but worries that she may need to put them in care while she works. She is struggling to help her children cope with losing their father while managing her own grief. And, as she and Carlos were high school sweethearts and married at 18, she also has to learn to define who she is now that she is single. Carolina is strong and resilient but she and her children will likely need several years of support before they are successfully transitioned. If we help her, everyone wins. If our systems on Main

Street fail Carolina, she and her children may enter a generational cycle of poverty which can be difficult to reverse.

While these families comprise a relatively small fraction of our post-9/11 military community, these women and their children are at the most serious risk for failure to thrive and long-term dependency on community systems for basic needs. They may be most in need of solid community support.

FEDERAL CONTRACTORS

There have been more than 500 contractors killed and 11,000 wounded post-9/11. Countless more suffer from the affects of Post-Traumatic Stress as a result of their work in the Green Zone or outside the wire (in combat situations). I bring this up as a brief side note because we are starting to see a trend for military-like physical and mental health issues surfacing in our civilian population who work to support America's wars in the Middle East.

Many of these contractors, as well as personnel in Federal agencies in the intelligence and homeland security sectors, are Veterans who have already deployed multiple times. So, a civilian job in the Green Zone or outside the wire "counts" as another deployment. These civilian deployments are often especially difficult for Veterans because they are back in theater but, out of uniform, they do not have the support of the "band of brothers" (or sisters). Their contractor status may heighten their sense of isolation.

> "Robert" served eight years in the Army, from 2003 to 2011. After separating from the Service, he bounced from one contracting job to another, sometimes in theater, sometimes elsewhere overseas. He struggled with PTSD, especially when he was out of the country. Lacking access to care and support, he went through periods of heavy drinking as a way to take the edge off the isolation, pain, and depression.

Robert had a serious mental health emergency when on assignment in India. His company had no plan for Robert's care and no protocols to bring him home. His father, a senior executive at a Fortune 50 company, was notified and was able to find a doctor in Mumbai who would essentially drug Robert and deliver him to the airport. Airline personnel, essentially treating Robert like an unaccompanied minor, shepherded him back to the U.S. where he could receive treatment.

The good news is that Robert came home to a loving family. He had the resources to get the in-patient treatment he needed. And, he had the self-awareness to recognize that this time he needed to get serious about getting help to heal. The challenge is that we will increasingly see cases like Robert's as we bring our military home and hire them into civilian contracting positions where they will be deployed back to high risk, high stress environments.

Many of you reading this little book work in these companies and agencies. As we transition from wars to reconstruction in the Middle East and as we face entanglements in other high risk environments, we are likely to see an increase in Veteran-like issues for contractors and Federal workers. A civilian deployment or overseas assignment to the Green Zone, or other high risk environments, is physically and psychologically indistinguishable to the human body. It is irrelevant whether a person is there in uniform or not. Many Veteran families and civilian employers do not seem to have put these facts together. Just one more of the almost limitless ways that America's wars in the Middle East will affect Hometown America for decades to come.

THEORY MADE (MOSTLY) SIMPLE

I know I promised from the beginning to keep this simple, so that a typical citizen can understand what's going on. But, there are a few theories, or what my friends and colleagues affectionately refer to as "Gretchen's big ideas," that I think help explain why our post-9/11 Veterans are having trouble transitioning. Much of what I am going to say here applies to non-Veterans who are going through major life changes, too, so I am guessing a lot of it will ring true to parts of your own life. The military piece just adds to the complexity of the picture.

PEOPLE ARE NOT PYRAMIDS

Some of you may remember reading about psychologist Abraham Maslow in high school. In the 1940s, he proposed what we now call "Maslow's Hierarchy of Needs," which has shaped our ideas about how human beings develop and transition.

Essentially, his theory says that first you must have the basics—air, water, food, and shelter. Once you have those things, you move on to address safety, employment, money, health, resources, and property. From there, you turn your attention to family, friends, sexual intimacy, and community. Once you have the basics, you can begin to work on self-confidence, self-esteem, achievement, and respect for yourself and others. Once you have mastered the first four levels, you can finally begin to focus on morality, creativity, open-mindedness, etc. This generally accepted hierarchy has shaped many social service programs. Get people food and housing; then get them a job; then work on their inter-personal relationships; and, finally, you can get them to think beyond their family to their community and the greater good.

Unfortunately, people are not pyramids and we do not live in levels. If you have known someone who lost their job, or perhaps that was

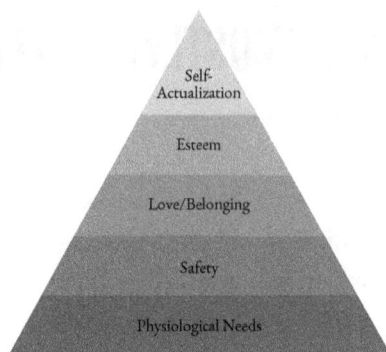

you, did they suddenly set aside all inter-personal relationships to focus on employment? Were they suddenly incapable of maintaining their religious practices or playing the piano? Of course not! People are not pyramids and as adults we cannot transition in programs that fail to address our 360° selves, as if adult transition is a series of karate belt tests. Just because we find ourselves lower on the pyramid does not mean we have forgotten who we used to be and how it used to feel to live higher up the pyramid.

In the work I have done with Homeward Deployed, we look at transition as a holistic process that takes into account an adult's 360° Self. Family well-being cannot be sequenced after employment transition and, in fact, they affect each other, as you will see shortly. A post-9/11 Veteran, Guard, or Reserve who had stable employment and a happy family life cannot just focus on a job hunt while ignoring the well-being of their family. The loss of sense of belonging upon separating from the military will affect the mental preparedness of a Service Member as they job hunt, begin a job on Main Street, or start college. The loss of self-esteem, self-confidence, and often self-respect for a newly disabled Veteran who can no longer function like they used to will impact relationships with a spouse or partner, family, and friends; this in turn can undermine rehabilitation, employment transition, or a return to school. Homeward Deployed's coaching philosophy is based not on a "hierarchy" but a "wholearchy" of interdependent needs which must be addressed simultaneously.

Transition work for adults must collapse Maslow's "hierarchy" in a way that recognizes that the levels are not stand-alone elements but inter-connected components of a process that, as you will soon see, is complex and sticky.

TRANSITION IS LIKE A SPIDER WEB...IT'S COMPLEX AND STICKY

Transition and reintegration for Veterans, Guard, Reserve, and their families is complex. It involves many systems that our post-9/11 military must navigate all at once. Do you remember learning about ecosystems in elementary school? Water evaporates from a lake and forms into clouds that eventually produce rain which replenishes the lake. But, if there is a lot of pollution in the air, the rain may become acid rain which not only causes our cars to rust faster but eventually pollutes the lake. The fish in the lake begin to absorb the pollutants, so when elderly people eat fish caught in the lake, they become sick. Meanwhile, the air pollution makes kids with asthma sicker so it's more likely that their parents drive them places, adding to the air pollution, which causes more acid rain, which further pollutes the lake, so the fish absorb more toxins, and now everyone gets sick eating the fish. Hopefully, I am smarter than a fifth grader and got that right!

Service Members and their families transition in a similar system that we can think of as a "Transition Ecosystem." Our biological ecosystem has subsystems like rain, pollution, fish, humans, and disease.

The transition ecosystem has subsystems that are the same for all people going through a major period life change, like job-seeking, family, housing, and education. The transition ecosystem for military also includes unique subsystems like acute medical care, mental health

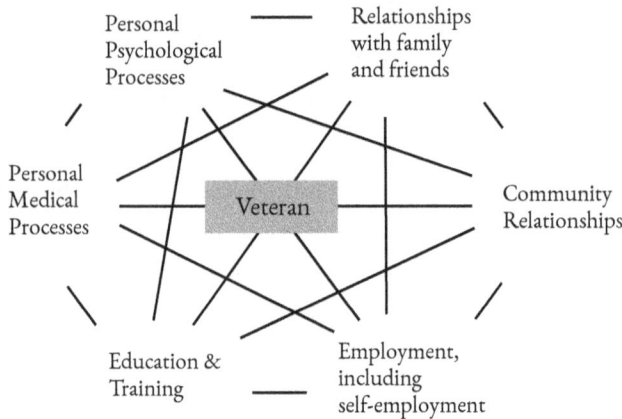

care, career change, and building new communities. And, these subsystems are all linked and they must all be navigated at the same time.

Why is this important? Consider the millions of Americans who are unemployed. Probably many of you reading this little book, like me, have found yourself unexpectedly unemployed at one time. So, what do you do? You spiff up your resume, you look at job postings, you send in resumes, and you apply for unemployment benefits if you are eligible. Perhaps you tell your friends you are looking so that they can keep their eyes out for someone who is hiring. Perhaps you attend networking events to meet potential employers. So, you are in an employment transition in your hometown, supported by family and friends, and probably cutting back on eating out or beach weekends.

Now consider a typical transitioning military. You were an 11 bravo, an infantryman, at Fort Hood, Texas, who earned $36,000 a year with $13,000 in a housing allowance for your family, plus full benefits. You thought you would have a 20 year career in the military. But, after eight years in the Army and four deployments, you cannot re-enlist because of the drawdown and you unexpectedly find yourself unemployed. To have a similar lifestyle, you need a job that pays $49,000 plus full benefits. You are 26 with a high school diploma.

You have no idea what you want to do. Everyone says that you should use your GI Bill and go back to school, but you don't know what you would study. You really want to find something to be passionate about, just like you were with your military career. Now that you're no longer an 11bravo, you are not exactly sure who you are.

Meanwhile, your wife says, "Listen, bub, I held down the fort for eight years while you spent 60 months deployed. I have been waiting four years to have another baby. You need to get a job." You went into the military at 18 after you graduated from high school and you have never written a resume, been on a job interview, or bought a suit. Unemployment in Texas has risen to 7.2%. Your wife wants to move home to California to be near family, but unemployment there is 10.7%. You two fight all the time about what you should do and where you should live.

Meanwhile, you have been struggling with back problems from the weight of your Kevlar vest and all the time you spent bouncing around in a humvee. You lost your best friend in Tikrit, Iraq, during your last deployment. He was shot in the chest and you held him as he bled to death. You've tried to be there for his 19 year old wife who just had a baby. You have nightmares most nights and every time you see his wife, it reminds you of the day he died. You haven't been able to get a VA rating and your friends tell you it could take two years to get one. Now that you are no longer active duty, you can't get counseling so you find yourself drinking most nights to take the edge off. You know you shouldn't but you don't know how else to manage your stress. You and your wife fight about your drinking, too. She is threatening to leave, which only increases your stress. You would get help if you could but you don't know where to go and help would have to be free because now you're living on unemployment pay and supporting a family.

So, what's the plan, Stan? What are you going to do? Where do you start? What's the first step? Transition is an ecosystem: it's complex and there are a lot of sticky issues that don't have easy solutions. As a result, as many as 70% of our young post-9/11 military and their families struggle with transition. (At the risk of shameless self-promotion, this is where Homeward Deployed's Transition Coaching is a great fit.)

It All Starts with Employment

When most people transition, no matter how strong or self-sufficient they are, they need support. In the best of all possible worlds, people in transition have access to positive support systems: family, friends, a community, housing, healthy food, stable employment, savings and/or investments, health insurance, medical care, counseling or therapy, good teachers, transportation, ways to manage stress, hobbies, pets, etc. Unfortunately, when a person does not have a positive support system, they will seek support from the negative support systems: smoking, binge eating, drinking, illicit drugs, misuse of prescription drugs, video game addiction, gang membership, accumulating debt, gambling, theft, physical violence, unhealthy sexual relations, etc.

It is absolutely not the case that America has "bad Veterans" (or "bad" Guard or Reserve). What we have are often very young people who lack the positive support systems to successfully navigate the entirety of the transition ecosystem all at the same time. And, many of these young people are not just transitioning themselves, they are

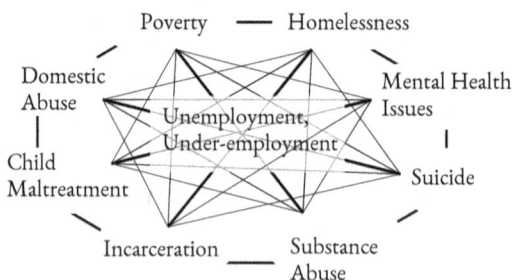

transitioning spouses, partners, children, and even elderly parents. And, many of these young people are making this huge transition while adjusting to a recent disability or serious mental health issue. Simply put, they are overwhelmed.

And, the big kahuna, the mother lode, the pink elephant in the room....is employment. Scientific research shows that unemployment and under-employment are connected to poverty, homelessness, mental health issues, suicide, substance abuse, domestic abuse, child maltreatment, and incarceration. This is true for all of us, not just transitioning military. And, these issues which are heavily impacting our transitioning military, are all a complex, interconnected, sticky web on their own.

For example, substance abuse makes you more likely to lose your job, find yourself homeless, feel depressed, think about or attempt suicide, commit domestic abuse, and end up incarcerated. Having mental health issues makes you more likely to lose your job, abuse substances, think about committing suicide, or find yourself homeless. Being homeless makes it hard to find and keep a job while increasing your risk for substance abuse, mental health issues, suicide, and becoming incarcerated or being a crime victim.

When you have a job, these issues are less likely to become a problem. If they do become a problem, they are likely to be less severe and/or of shorter duration. And, with financial stability, you have the resources to address them through health insurance, employee assistance programs, or money from your paycheck. That is why employment is one of the most important factors in the equation to prevent our post-9/11 military from turning from positive support systems to the negative support systems.

You Can Never Go Home Again

As a trained anthropologist, I must include a brief detour into the significance of military culture on transition. Fair warning, this is one of "Gretchen's Big Ideas" that is not widely discussed. Those who know me well shake their heads when I say, "Hey! I've been thinking...."

Becoming a Service Member and returning "home" is a process of cultural transition and reintegration. Yes, it all takes place with an American passport, but the return home can bring out a form of "culture shock." If you have ever lived outside the U.S. for an extended period and returned "home," you will know exactly what I mean. If you ever see me speak, ask me about my experience buying toilet paper after returning from Honduras.

While we do have laws and shared standards that guide our behavior on Main Street, the structures that shape military culture are all-encompassing. Enlisted and officers alike must adhere to strict guidelines dictating uniforms, haircuts, eyeglasses, body piercings, tattoos, cosmetics, and jewelry. Especially enlisted have little or no choice in where they are posted, how often they move, where they can live, who they can live with (if you live on base), and when they are deployed. Depending on where they are posted, they may not be allowed to bring a spouse or children. They may have little or no choice as to their military occupational specialty, regardless of what was promised upon enlistment. They must obey strict protocols in how to relate to people above and below them in the hierarchy, including who they can have personal relationships with. Orders from a commanding officer must be obeyed absolutely. Failure to use alcohol wisely, dating the wrong person, and/or mismanaging marital relationships can lead to demotion, dishonorable discharge, or even a court martial and jail time.

The process of boot camp alters a recruit's individual sense of identity and autonomy, reshaping the independent, thinking Self into the interdependent, dutiful Team Member necessary for unit cohesion and survival in combat. Decision-making is top down and orders are to be obeyed absolutely; this is the model of teamwork necessary for survival in combat. Over and over again, I hear Veterans talk about how active duty Service promotes a culture of dependency. An Army wife complained, "They even call us (spouses) dependents. I am 40 years old with a college education. I am not a dependent, I am an equal." From an organizational development perspective, the military has an optimal structure to maintain discipline and win wars.

Suddenly, a Service Member is back "home" and in transition, often with a family in tow. They may have lived on Main Street, they took an oath that they would die to defend Hometown America, but in a sense they were visitors there because their primary culture was the military. At first, the ability to make decisions can seem freeing and empowering, but having seemingly limitless choices can quickly become overwhelming. There are almost no limits to where to live or what career to pursue. They can wear whatever they want, but they must fit into civilian expectations that are not clearly spelled out anywhere. They can interact with anyone they want at any time, but they are still constrained by standards of behavior; the problem is that beyond legal constraints, these behavior standards on Main Street are invisible. Wearing a T-shirt to a business mixer and calling everyone "sir" or "ma'am" is not necessarily going to smooth the way in a job transition.

In comparison to the military culture of entitlements, Main Street can seem downright alien. Many jobs, especially in today's economic climate, do not come with health care, let alone full benefits. While some businesses offer military discounts, the prices on Main Street are often the cause of sticker shock for Service Members used to shopping at the commissary and exchange. It is difficult if not impossible to replace the high quality, heavily subsidized childcare available on most military installations.

On top of seemingly harsh realities (hey, those of us on Main Street have always lived with these realities), team is gone, replaced by a sense of isolation. The honeymoon phase of reunions is replaced by a lingering sense for many Veterans that they no longer fit in. Again, being young and lacking life perspective, the civilians on Main Street are labeled "unfriendly" or "uncaring," when the sense of unease comes from inside themselves. While basic training created the interdependent, dutiful Team Member necessary for unit cohesion, even Transition GPS is not designed to restore the independent, thinking Self necessary to thrive on Main Street.

Whether they spent four years straight out of high school as an enlisted Service Member or thirty years of service retiring as a general, it can be jarring and disillusioning to discover that "home" does not feel like "home." This is particularly true for young transitioning military who lack life perspective and frame this experience as Main Street being "anti-Veteran," rather than realizing that as we mature, we all go through these transitions. It's a process called life.

HOW RECRUITMENT IMPACTS TRANSITION

As someone who has worked in underserved communities, I must include a brief detour into the significance of military recruitment on transition. This is another one of "Gretchen's Big Ideas" which actually gives people cause to think. And, I'll warn you it may seem a bit controversial on the surface.

I believe our recruitment patterns are in large part responsible for the epidemic of Post-Traumatic Stress Disorder (PTSD) and Military Sexual Trauma (MST). I know that's a bold statement. Here's the logic....

The general buzz today is that America's military is the best educated, best prepared fighting force America has ever had. But, I know that the military recruits heavily from under-served and rural communities. In order to meet recruitment quotas, standards were lowered to allow enlistment of young people who lacked a high school diploma or had criminal records. How could these two things both be true, I wondered? Finally a colleague and friend who was the senior enlisted for his Service explained this to me. Until about 2008, when the economy began to decline, the military did in fact recruit heavily from underserved and rural communities, often lowering recruitment standards. When the economy collapsed, the military became an attractive option for a different segment of the population. Thus, we arrive at the best educated, best prepared fighting force America has ever had coupled with a large population of military now transitioning out who come from and return home to under-served and rural communities.

I worked with at-risk/at promise youth "East of the River" in Washington DC for two years, exactly the people who we recruited into the military for years after Vietnam. ("East of the River" is DC's version of Harlem or East L.A.) We estimated that as many as 70% of the children in our program had PTSD from living in a high violence, high crime community. We had a six year old who had witnessed three people shot to death and had no access to any counseling. So, as the military recruited from these communities, they built a fighting force that came to military service with significant rates of pre-existing PTSD. Then these Service Members were put through boot camp, which is an intense psychological process. Then, they were put through multiple deployments, which layered trauma on trauma. So, it is not surprising to me that we have an epidemic of military PTSD, it's predictable. Many of these young people should never have been accepted into the military. And, as we now face finding solutions to the epidemic of military PTSD, it is going to require therapeutic approaches that incorporate helping adults to process childhood traumas and attachment/bonding disorders, not just military trauma.

As for MST, many boys and young men grow up in underserved and rural communities without positive male role models. When I worked East of the River, roughly 90% of our youth had no father figure in their lives. Their idols were rapper Chris Brown (who beat his girlfriend, Rihanna), Michael Vick (who tortured dogs as part of a dog fighting scandal), and OJ Simpson (who apparently beat the system by fending off murder charges). Local drug gangs were both feared and admired; they had lots of money and guns....they ruled the neighborhood. Add to that societal messages, both overt and subliminal, that encourage unhealthy ideas about masculinity and the treatment of women. It's a recipe for disaster. It's not that these are "bad" youth, they are boys and young men who are not offered the support of positive male role models, so they turn to the only male role models available.

Many if not most of the women I worked with who lived East of the River had been raped, often as young teens and sometimes more than once. I was often asked how old I was the first time I was raped. They were shocked that I have never been raped. So, rape was simply "what happened" to girls and women.

Now, imagine that those young men are given uniforms, salaries, and guns—not bad young men, but young men with no positive male role models and mothers who accepted rape and assault as a way of life. Now they have the power that they dreamed of as boys, coupled with unhealthy ideas about masculinity and how to treat women. So, again, it is not surprising to me that we have an epidemic of MST, it's predictable. And, changing this culture will not just require better leadership and policies from the top, it will require some intensive work at the bottom to change cultural beliefs and norms.

I know this is a lot to digest, and may be hard for you to read. However, unless we address problems in a direct manner, and name the pink elephants in the room, we will never find solutions to help this generation of Veterans transition well. And, if we do that job well, there will undoubtedly be lessons learned that prevent the issues that we are seeing in our post-9/11 military from happening with our military moving forward.

THE BAD THINGS THAT HAPPEN TO GOOD VETERANS (AND THEIR FAMILIES)

Traumatic Brain Injury (TBI)

Traumatic Brain Injury (TBI) and Post-Traumatic Stress Disorder (PTSD) are the signature wounds of America's wars on terror. More than 250,000 Service Members, roughly 10% of all of our post-9/11 military, have been diagnosed with some form of TBI.

Mild TBI, often called concussions on Main Street, account for 70 to 90% of all TBIs. Symptoms of mild TBI include physical symptoms like headaches, nausea, vomiting, fatigue, blurred vision, sensitivity to light or noise, balance problems, and sleep disturbance; cognitive symptoms like trouble concentrating, short-term memory loss, trouble processing information, and impaired judgment; and behavioral/emotional symptoms like irritability, agitation, depression, anxiety, impulsiveness, and aggression.

Recovery time usually takes one to three months for mild TBI. About 90% of all mild TBIs heal on their own with rest but the remaining 10% may require rehabilitation for full recovery. Having one TBI, even a mild TBI, increases your risk for a more severe TBI if you have another injury. What does that mean? It means that if a person with a previous TBI is in a car accident or gets hurt playing football, they are more likely to have another TBI than someone who has never had a TBI. That second TBI may be more serious, moderate instead of mild, because that person's brain has already been damaged once.

Tony was a high school football player. He was proud of the fact that he had been knocked out once and had to be carried off the field. His bravado helped him earn an assignment in artillery. He witnessed several IED explosions. Several months into his deployment, Tony started to get headaches. He had trouble sleeping and concentrating while on duty. Normally the eternal optimist, he became irritable and depressed. His commanding officer suggested he talk to the chaplain about his combat stress. When Tony started to wear sunglasses in the mess hall, complained about needing glasses, and started a fistfight with one of his buddies, Tony was sent for a medical check-up where he was diagnosed with a mild TBI.

As medical knowledge has improved, we are learning that the percussive impact of an IED blast can travel a mile away. What does that mean? It means that a soldier a mile away from an IED explosion could end up with a mild TBI. The Defense Centers of Excellence estimated at a briefing in 2012 that we may have another 200,000+ undiagnosed mild TBIs in our post-9/11 Veteran population. We have also learned that mild TBIs cannot be detected by traditional CT scans and MRIs. It takes a special MRI called diffusion tensor imaging to detect these mild TBIs (there's a reason I am burdening you with this medical term).

Why am I telling you all of this? My concern is that we almost certainly have large numbers of Veterans, as well as members of the Guard/Reserve who deploy to and from their homes, with undiagnosed mild TBIs home on Main Street. They may be misdiagnosed as having combat stress or reintegration issues and get referred for counseling. For the 90%, things will eventually get better on their own and counseling never hurts. But, what happens to the 10% who need medical intervention to heal? Because their TBIs are undiagnosed or misdiagnosed, and require a very special and expensive form of MRI to detect, they are not receiving the medical care they need for recovery. The window of opportunity for recovery is closing. And, they are unknowingly at additional risk for moderate or severe TBI should they sustain another TBI. Please, remember this if there are transitioning military in your sphere of influence. You may be their lifeline to proper medical attention and healing. Would you suspect an undetected mild TBI in Amanda's story?

Amanda was delivering supplies when the humvee ahead of her hit an IED. It was scary and one of her friends was injured, but Amanda thought she was fine. This was her second deployment; IEDs were no big deal and she was safe. She was focused on getting home and finalizing plans for her wedding.

Amanda returned home ten days later. Her employer, a Marine Veteran, had honored his promise that her job would be waiting for her when she got home from her Guard deployment. He even had a party for her. Once a star employee, Amanda repeatedly forgot things her boss asked her to do and misplaced paperwork. She snapped at the other employees and even stormed out of the office in the middle of a staff meeting.

Amanda constantly complained to her fiance about headaches. She had trouble keeping food down and began to lose weight. He was afraid she was pregnant, but she assured him she wasn't. He noticed that they seemed to go through a lot of beer but, when he confronted her about her drinking, she denied that she was drinking more than a can a night. She also started shopping, coming home from work almost every night with a pair of shoes, a little gift for him, or decorations for the wedding. This from a woman who dreaded going to the mall to shop at Christmas.

Moderate and severe TBI, can permanently impact a Service Member's career, family, and life goals. Symptoms may include blindness, hearing impairment, loss of speech functions, and long-term memory loss as well as more intense experiencing of the symptoms of mild TBI. Recovery for moderate and severe TBI may take up to two years, with full recovery often not possible. Life beyond the initial rehabilitation period may include cycles of loss and recovery. Lifelong care-taking is often required and continuing access to rehabilitative services may be critical to maintaining progress achieved in recovery. Remember the story of our anonymous referral from the Wounded Warrior Project? TBI also increases the risk of epilepsy, Alzheimer's, and Parkinson's in the long-term.

So, what is the potential cost of this to Main Street? The Congressional Budget Office estimates that it costs $11,700 per Veteran for the first year of treatment for TBI, not including acute care. Let's be generous and assume that the 30% of military with moderate or severe TBI actually receive services from the military. We are left with 175,000 Service Members with diagnosed mild TBIs, 70% of Veterans refusing to use the VA for services and a two year wait just to get a VA rating that gives you eligibility for services. Now factor in another 200,000 with undiagnosed mild TBI, 10% of whom will require treatment and will seek that care on Main Street. The cost of treating 136,500 transitioning military on Main Street could come with a price tag of $1.6B for a single year of treatment. Costs will decline in subsequent years but the total budget bottom line to communities will continue to increase. Now, imagine that we fail to address the needs of these Veterans and $1.6B in prevention turns into $14.4B in remedial care (remember how $1 of prevention is worth $9 of cure?).

Are you beginning to see the long-term dollar value of mobilizing on Main Street and finding the money to make sure our military members transition well? Remember, even the $14.4B figure doesn't account for military wives needing help for domestic abuse, kids arriving in school so stressed they require special services from the public schools, or families who end up homeless or live in poverty because of divorce or suicide. My apologies if this sounds depressing but it is a potential reality. And, it's largely avoidable if we mobilize now.

Post-Traumatic Stress Disorder (PTSD)

Post-Traumatic Stress Disorder (PTSD) and Traumatic Brain Injury (TBI) are the signature wounds of America's wars on terror. PTSD is a mental health condition triggered by exposure to a terrifying event, most often associated with war. What most people don't realize is that many of us as civilians experience trauma at some point in our lives, and some of us will develop PTSD. It is estimated that 60%

of men and 50% of women at some point experience trauma....rape, assault, domestic abuse, child abuse, a serious car accident, witnessing a violent crime, industrial accidents....with 30% of men and 25% of women experiencing multiple traumas over a lifetime. But, witnessing trauma does not always result in PTSD. It is estimated that when exposed to trauma only 8% of men and 20% of women will develop some form of PTSD.

> Sophia was the passenger in a car driven by her best friend. Driving through an intersection, they were broadsided by a drunk driver and Sophia witnessed her friend being instantly killed. Sophia was uninjured but she cried uncontrollably for weeks, suffered from intense nightmares, and became so depressed she couldn't get out of bed. Initially, she refused to travel by car and to this day she refuses to drive in spite of holding a valid driver's license. Sophia has steadfastly refused treatment for PTSD, although persistent symptoms have existed for more than a decade.

Common reactions immediately following trauma exposure include feelings of fear and anxiety; nightmares and other sleep disturbances; difficulty concentrating; frequently reviewing the details of the trauma; and feeling on edge or jittery. It is important to remember that these are all NORMAL human reactions. These reactions are only the basis for a diagnosis of PTSD when they do not go away. Other common reactions, which are normal but may indicate entry into the PTSD spectrum, include emotions of sadness, grief, or depression; feeling numb, disconnected, or withdrawn; feeling angry, guilty, or ashamed; avoiding things that are reminders of the trauma (i.e. avoiding crowds, driving, going out at night); and shifting how you see yourself and/or the world to a more negative perspective (i.e. "No one cares" or "This makes me a bad person").

With our military coming home, Service Members are more likely to develop PTSD following trauma if they have had multiple or lengthier deployments; have had more combat exposure (i.e. infantry soldier vs. supply chain); are members of the Guard/Reserve or Veterans; or are enlisted, female or Hispanic. In talking to hundreds of post-9/11 military over the years, there is a consistent pattern in how they describe deployments:

> "I was fine after my first deployment; I just had some challenges transitioning back home. It was harder after my second deployment. After my third deployment, it was really bad." Now consider that there are military who have deployed six or eight times.
>
> Military wives tell a different story: "Even after his first deployment, things were rough. He was moody, edgy, impatient with me and the kids. He would get angry easily. He would toss and turn all night, have nightmares. It took about six or eight months to get back to what felt normal."

PTSD is often related to other conditions. Not surprisingly, people with PTSD are more likely to have depression, anger management issues, substance abuse problems, and difficulties in personal and work relationships. They are more at risk for suicide. They are more likely to be unemployed or have difficulties on the job. Traumatic Brain Injury (TBI) and PTSD go hand-in-hand.

Recovery from trauma, and reducing the incidence of PTSD, depends heavily on the nature of the traumatic event; the severity of the initial reaction to the trauma; the strength of a person's support system, both in the immediate and the long-term; pre-existing stress or new stress while recovering; the reactions of a person's social network (i.e. judgment vs. compassion); and substance abuse. By mobilizing to make sure support systems are strong, and by educating civilians about the experiences of Veterans, we increase the likelihood that our military will transition well.

Counseling or therapy can be important for PTSD recovery but we know that fewer than 50% of our transitioning military get the help that they need. There is a culture of being "Army Strong," where asking for help is a sign of weakness. There are very real and legitimate fears of being stigmatized or denied promotions. Organizations like Give an Hour provide confidential counseling outside the system. And, we are seeing an increase in transitioning military and their families using traditional community mental health services for reasons of confidentiality or because care is not available through military channels.

Jeremy has been in the Army for ten years with three deployments in the infantry. He is up for promotion. His girlfriend says he has all the signs of PTSD. Who wouldn't after 45 months of combat? He's worried because he has caught himself distracted from his duties; he's afraid he will make a mistake and someone will get hurt. Jeremy admits he needs help but he refuses to see a military counselor, in spite of greater acceptance of therapy by military leadership, for fear it will affect his promotion. Since he isn't religious, he doesn't feel comfortable talking to a chaplain. He doesn't want to private pay for confidential counseling in his civilian community, even though he has the money and his parents would happily contribute. He also questions whether a civilian therapist could really understand what he's been through.

The widely respected 2010 RAND study found that the rates of PTSD reported in studies for today's military range from 1% to 60%. Yes, that's a pretty big range! A 2012 Institute of Medicine report narrows that range to 13% to 20%. But, a 2012 VA report shows that 29% of post-9/11 Veterans receiving care at the VA have diagnosed PTSD. And, a Harvard study suggests that the rate of PTSD actually stands between 2.1% and 13.8% (it's Harvard, they can use the decimal points!). So, how do we make sense of this? Since this isn't a research project, let's take a midpoint for all these numbers and say that at any given time 15% of transitioning military are coping with PTSD.

So, what is the potential cost of this to Main Street? The Congressional Budget Office estimates that it costs $8,300 per Veteran for the first year of treatment for PTSD. If we have 3.2M Veterans, 15% of whom have PTSD at any given time, costing $8,300 per person for treatment, we arrive at a total cost of $4B for PTSD care in the first year. Given that 70% of Veterans refuse to use the VA for services or endure up to a two year wait just to get a VA rating that gives them eligibility for services, the price tag for Main Street could be $2.8B for first year care. If we fail to address the needs of these Veterans, $2.8B in prevention turns into $25.2B in remedial care. Again, this doesn't include the cost of impact on families, employers, police, court systems, etc. Food for thought, if you're not already a bit queasy.

POLYTRAUMA

Polytrauma literally means multiple injuries. Often involving TBI, PTSD, or both, the widespread use of IEDs makes it a signature diagnosis for Service Members in our wars against terror. Common polytrauma diagnoses for our post-9/11 military include: amputation, TBI, and PTSD; spinal cord injury, TBI, and PTSD; TBI, PTSD, and blindness; TBI, PTSD, and hearing impairment; TBI, severe burns, and PTSD.

While not every Service Member who is injured develops PTSD, they are correlated. Physical injury doubles the rate of PTSD; half of Wounded Warriors with three or more injuries suffer from serious PTSD.

SECONDARY PTSD

Then there is secondary PTSD, which is increasing at alarming rates for military spouses and partners, Wounded Warrior care-givers, and military children. This form of PTSD comes from secondary exposure to trauma: seeing news reports of troops killed and worrying that your deployed loved one is among them; supporting a spouse, friend, or child through trauma; care-giving an injured, ill, or wounded Service Member; attending military funerals; supporting a friend who is care-giving or has lost a spouse; worrying that your parent will not come home from combat; growing up in a home with someone in mental health care or with a serious disability; etc. There is valid concern that Secondary PTSD is over-diagnosed as a catchall term for care-giver stress, deployment stress, and normal life stress. While we cannot yet pinpoint numbers, our military families are, nonetheless, struggling with serious and often debilitating stress regardless of the label.

Kate, a stay-at-home mom, and her four-year-old son, Josh, could hardly wait for daddy to come home. Just three more weeks of a 15-month deployment according to the jelly bean jar! Unfortunately, Andy was injured in an IED explosion two weeks before he was scheduled to come home. He suffered a moderate TBI, severe burns to his face and upper body, and partial blindness.

Kate and Josh spent months living at Fisher House near the hospital. As the severity of Andy's injuries became obvious, Kate struggled to accept his disfigurements and changes to his personality. As she learned more about the explosion, she had nightmares where she saw Andy being blown up. She began to have panic attacks as she thought about having to go to work and leaving Josh in daycare. She wondered whether they would ever have a sex life again and she became anxious about whether having another baby might be out of the question, especially if she had to go to work.

The first time he saw his daddy, Josh was afraid and ran out of the room. He worried constantly because mommy cried so much and she never wanted to play race cars with him like she used to. He started wetting his pants. He became aggressive with the other kids in his preschool and was eventually asked not to return. Eventually, Kate and Josh were able to get services from an early childhood therapist who helped them to establish a new normal. But, case workers worried about whether they could find services when they moved back home to their small town in a rural area to be near family.

Many, if not most, of these military family members who choose to seek services will look to community mental health because they have little or no eligibility through traditional military channels. Consider that by 2020 we may have 6M to 7M military family members. If 15% of them need care for secondary PTSD at $8,300 each, the cost of care on Main Street would be $7.5B just for PTSD care. You can argue with the numbers and assumptions but clearly community mental health on Main Street is potentially facing a huge unbudgeted need for care.

We also see secondary PTSD in the counselors, medical personnel, and other support service people who work with our transitioning military. How many of them are there? What if 15% of them need care from our community mental health services? This is starting to sound like an ad for Anthony Bourdain's "Parts Unknown"....more food for thought.

MORAL INJURY

Moral injury, like PTSD, is a form of psychological trauma. However, it is not triggered by exposure to trauma but by the violation of deeply held moral and ethical beliefs or expectations through direct action, witnessing of actions, or by association. These transgressions cause profound feelings of guilt (betrayal of the Self) and shame (betrayal of society). It can also result from a sense of betrayal by trusted authority figures. Moral injury is a deep spiritual crisis not a psychiatric disorder, although it can trigger PTSD, addictive behaviors, depression, and suicide.

> Patriotism wasn't always a challenging issue for Hamid. He was proud of his new country, having left Iran with his family as a child. His parents approved of the U.S. involvement in the Gulf War to free Kuwait. He enlisted in the Air Force after graduating from high school and earned citizenship while in the Service.

After 9/11, Hamid became deeply troubled by the anti-Muslim feelings so openly expressed by his fellow airmen. He had never been open about being a devout Muslim but now he felt compelled to hide his religion. He also struggled to understand how Islam had been so perverted by the Taliban and Al-qaeda. And, he was so deeply troubled by the jihadist talk among the older men at his mosque that he stopped going, abandoning what had once been an important social support.

Like his friends, Hamid shared the desire to avenge American deaths. But, he began to question his orders as he was deployed and assigned to bombing runs over Iraq. He knew that the bombings would terrify, maim, and kill innocent civilians....people just like his cousins who still lived in Iran. Seeing Iraqi children with missing limbs, he became obsessed with guilt and shame, certain that it was his bombs that were responsible. Witnessing the poverty in Iraq, and then Afghanistan, made him wonder what his life might be like if he had grown up in such extreme poverty with no pathway out. After retiring from the Service, Hamid finds some peace by working with The Mission Continues and Team Rubicon.

Moral injury has only very recently been recognized as a factor impacting military transition, although its roots clearly go back to the Vietnam War. The reality of war is that killing changes you forever. Witnessing atrocities changes you forever. The inability to save your buddies or prevent innocent civilians from dying changes you forever. These are the realities of war, any war. These are realities that we don't like to talk about. Civilians are uncomfortable being exposed to the realities of war, experiencing a sense of complicity in the actions of the soldiers who fight our nation's wars. Our warriors are afraid or ashamed to reveal the realities of war, for fear that we could never forgive them or that we will think less of them. And, unlike World War II where there was a clear enemy and a real threat, Vietnam and our recent wars against terror are much more morally ambiguous.

"Frank" grew up in a blue collar town in the Midwest. His dad died when he was an infant and acceptance to West Point was a ticket out. A retired general, Frank spent more than 30 years in the military. He fought in most of the hotspots where America had a military presence, including countries where we were peacekeepers. Over the course of his career, he estimates that he personally killed hundreds of people; as a flag officer, he guesses his orders resulted in thousands of deaths, including civilian casualties.

A devout Catholic, he believes that he will go to Hell because God could never forgive him for what he has done. He is certain that the good things he has done in his life....taking care of his elderly mother, raising his son alone, his devotion to his men, his contributions to charity, his work on nonprofit boards....could never atone for the things he did in war. He is ashamed to talk to his priest, certain that he would never be able to understand the life of a soldier.

Frank is struggling to make sense of his life, to understand how he ended up with so much blood on his hands. While he can justify his actions in places like Somalia, he is haunted by the brutality of genocide he saw there. He deeply questions the wars in Iraq and Afghanistan. He berates himself for not questioning orders while he was on active duty. He wonders why he stayed in for so long, why he didn't see the reality of what he was doing earlier. He tells his girlfriend that he is a bad man and that she needs to find a good man to be with, because she is clearly a good person. His intense pain is heart wrenching.

Supporting Veterans through the journey of moral injury requires a spiritual not a psychological or psychiatric response. Moral injury is best healed through focused conversations with spiritual leaders and those trained to directly address moral, ethical, and spiritual beliefs that underlie often invisible cultural rules. Our spiritual leaders, coaches, mentors, military families, and others who help America's soldiers in transition need a forum to learn about moral injury, to find ways to effectively talk to our warriors, and to build the courage it takes to have deeply painful conversations. Helping our warriors heal from moral injury is a key to transition resilience. And, it will happen on Main Street.

MILITARY SEXUAL TRAUMA

Would it shock you to know that a female solider is more likely to be raped BY A PEER than she is to be killed in combat? Did you know that 10% of the victims of MST are men? Would it surprise you to know that there have been hundreds of cases of sexual assault, including rape, in VA hospitals? Would you be appalled if I told you that Dr. Kay Whitley, then the director of the Pentagon's Sexual Assault Prevention and Response Office, actually pitched an intervention program called, "Wait Until She's Sober?"

What if I told you that a 1950 Supreme Court ruling defined rape as an "alleged harm" that is "incident to" military service? In other words, rape by a fellow soldier is simply a routine risk of military service for soldiers. This ruling protects the Department of Defense from law suits brought by rape victims accusing the military of failing to address the appalling rates of military rape. To date, every court case challenging this ruling has been dismissed. Let that sink in a minute. In 1950, the Supreme Court classified rape as a normal part of military service and in the 21st century no court has been willing to explore whether this classification of rape should be challenged.

> "Janet" was a lawyer with the Judge Advocate General Corps, often
> known simply as JAG. As MST became a more challenging issue for the
> Pentagon, Janet was exclusively assigned to work with female soldiers who
> had reported being raped. Janet was routinely forced by her superiors at
> JAG to intimidate these women into recanting their rape accusations. Janet
> eventually had a nervous breakdown and was medically retired from the
> military. The diagnosis she received was secondary PTSD.

Military Sexual Trauma (MST) refers to psychological trauma experienced by Service Members as a result of rape, sexual assault, or sexual harassment. The Pentagon revealed in 2011 that there were 3,191 military sexual assaults reported; only about 10% of those cases ever went to trial. Their own report suggests that this number represents just 13.5% of the estimated 19,000 actual assaults that occurred that year.

Organizations that work with victims of MST have done surveys revealing much higher numbers: 27% of women in the military are raped in combat by a peer and 67% suffer sexual harassment and other forms of sexual assault with fewer than 1% of perpetrators ever being sentenced. Amy Ziering, producer of "The Invisible War," an award winning documentary on military rape, poignantly describes her experiences working with victims of military rape in a February 2013 interview with "Vanity Fair:"

> "[Rape in the military is] the number one cause of homelessness in our women veterans. The vast majority are not uplifting stories. I've been so haunted, honestly, by the level of the debilitation of these women, who were cut short so early in life, and in such a way that they couldn't ever recuperate and again reintegrate into society in any way.
>
> After we finished the film, I made this promise that I would try and find a way to physically help some of these women that I really was very worried about. A lot of the homes we visited, all the shades were drawn for years. Children would grow up in these dark homes, because that's the only way these women feel safe."

We need to remember that these women and their families are coming home, too. Given the intense victimization and betrayal they experienced by the military, they are less likely to pursue help from the VA. Community mental health and public schools may be the only safety net for these vulnerable women and their children. Would your community be prepared?

You may have heard that a soldier is more likely to die by suicide than s/he is to die in combat. You may have heard about the epidemic of military suicide. We now lose almost one active duty Service Member every day to suicide. The Army created Comprehensive Soldier Family Fitness. Resilience programs, formerly called Battlemind Training, were revised. Yet, in spite of 900 programs to prevent military suicide, the rate continues to rise. While Veterans account for only 8% of the population, they account for 20% of all suicides. The rate of Service Member and Veteran suicides now stands at 22 people per day. Joseph Bobrow, founder of the Coming Home Project, wrote in his Huffington Post Blog about Clay Hunt's stunning suicide death:

> "What shocked so many is that Clay was 'the poster boy' for how someone 'should' return from war. He 'did all the right things.' After coming home, he became proactive, helping create Team Rubicon and participated actively in Ride 2 Recovery. In 2010 he stormed the hill with IAVA, advocating and using his own experience to help others as part of their Ad Council Mental Health PSA program. He sought help at the VA, took his meds, tried to revive his sense of purpose through meaningful public service, had good friendships, and exercised vigorously. How then could Clay Hunt take his life?"

You might think that the highest rates of suicide would be among combat soldiers recently returned from deployment. Surprisingly, the highest suicide rates are among non-deployed National Guard. In recent Congressional testimony, the Pentagon has admitted that it will need to create a major cultural shift that reduces the stigma of coming forward for mental health care if it is going to effectively address the issue of military suicide.

This sounds like it should be strictly a Pentagon problem, doesn't it? But, our military suicides leave behind thousands of family members who require support services on Main Street. We are also seeing an alarming increase in the rate of suicides among military spouses. I know of at least one death of a care-giver, a mother who killed herself in her son's hospital room at Walter Reed. The person who told me the story gasped and said, "I never should have told you that happened." And, then there's the upward trend of "death by cop," where a Service Member engages law enforcement in a violent confrontation ending in death:

> January 16, 2013, Dustin Wernli called Tuscon, Arizona, 911 and asked police to shoot him. Officers responded and talked to Wernli for about 15 minutes. Wernli pulled a gun and was fatally shot by officers. Wernli was a combat medic who had suffered a TBI and was being treated for PTSD.

I cannot give you any statistics here because military families don't fall strictly under any agency's watch, so no one counts their deaths. Sad but true. Kristina Kauffman, executive director at Code of Support, talks about her friend, Faye Vick, who killed herself and her children by carbon monoxide poisoning:

> "When you know that you are the anchor — and if you go down, the family's going down — the problem is that you can only do that for so long," said Kaufmann. "That population (of spouses) is at the most risk. Because the storm is going to happen when everybody comes home. That's where we are, unfortunately, going to see an uptick in lots of negative outcomes, including suicide, including suicide among the spouses."

Did that sink in? "When everyone comes home." That would be now and in the years to come. We are at the stage where the water is receding out to sea before the tsunami hits.

Did you know that the single most important factor in suicide prevention is having someone to talk to? It's true for everyone, not just military. People who are truly intent on killing themselves don't talk about it. But, those who are thinking about it but want help will reach out to someone. And, 90% of the time, that "someone" is not going to be a counselor or therapist, it is going to be a spouse or significant other, a parent or sibling, a buddy or co-worker. In other words, someone just like you.

As a society, we don't like to talk about death. We especially don't like to talk about suicide. It's extremely confronting when someone you love tells you they want to kill themselves. I know, I've been there more than once. But, it is a teachable skill and many states offer free suicide prevention training for communities. If we want to break the cycle of military suicide, without waiting for the Pentagon to create "a major cultural shift," we can do that with education on Main Street and a healthy dose of personal courage.

Oh, and then there's the cost. The CDC estimates that a suicide costs $1.1M in medical expenses and lost productivity. With 22 suicides a day, that's a cost to communities of $24.2M every day and $8.8B every year in military suicide. And, how do we put a price tag on the human cost of spouses becoming widows or widowers, children losing a parent and even becoming orphans?

And, hating to bring up yet another sticky issue (but you should know me pretty well by now)....it's about gun control. As you know, 90% of transitioning military and Veterans are men. Men most often commit suicide using guns; we know this is true for the military because they even commissioned a study to look at this issue. States that have enacted waiting periods for gun purchases have seen their suicide rates go down dramatically. So, when you advocate against waiting periods and closing gun show loopholes, you are actually advocating in favor of policies which make it easier for Veterans (and everyone else) in your community to commit suicide by gun. That's a hard reality, I know. Just more food for thought.

Surprisingly, homelessness is one area where remarkable progress has been made in supporting our Veterans. On any given night in 2012, there were on average more than 60,000 homeless Veterans. That is a large number but the good news is that this is a 7% decline from 2011 and a 17% decline from 2009. But the battle isn't won yet and, as you will see below, there are reasons for concern that these numbers may climb if we don't mobilize at the community level now. And, homelessness is one issue that is almost always directly addressed at the community level, although funding may come from State or Federal government.

What we know is that about 80% of newly homeless Veterans have diagnosed mental disorders. Veterans with PTSD or TBI are three times as likely to end up homelessness. It is important to note that they were diagnosed BEFORE they became homeless. Roughly 4% of our post-9/11 Veterans end up homeless at least once in their first five years home. Surprisingly, most of the newly homeless do not become homeless right after coming home; they become homeless in the fourth or fifth year after coming home. What does all this mean? It means we have a window of opportunity to help people heal and find a pathway to transition well before they become homeless. "We" meaning communities because Veterans are on our watch, not the Pentagon's.

Maurice was raised by his grandmother. He enlisted in the Army and served eight years, including three deployments. Shortly after returning home and registering for college, his grandmother died. Maurice was forced to move out of their apartment in a rent-controlled building for seniors. Having no other family and not enough money to pay for his own apartment, he couch hopped among friends for many months. He got on the waiting list for a HUD voucher, but he was told it might be a three or four year wait. Eventually, he ran out of friends and ended up on the streets.

As a single young man, he was not a priority for a bed in a shelter. But, without basic food and shelter, Maurice is at risk for dropping out of school. That's a lose-lose proposition for everyone.

Poverty and serious illness often cause homelessness. Homelessness, especially for our female Veterans, is often caused by domestic abuse or other family crises. The impacts of MST often lead to homelessness for our female Veterans. And, many of our female Veterans have children in tow. Once homeless, people are at greater risk for substance abuse and addiction, developing or escalating mental health issues, suicide, malnutrition, serious illness including HIV and hepatitis, assault, rape, murder, and incarceration.

JJ enlisted in the Coast Guard to get away from an abusive home and a small town where she knew she had no future. She was so excited at the chance to travel the world. She was raped by her commanding officer, who kept her working late one night until they were alone. His buddies warned her not to report it, or there would be consequences. She developed mental health issues, started neglecting her duties, was repeatedly written up, and eventually received an "other than honorable" discharge.

With nowhere to go once she got home, and no benefits, she ended up on the streets. After a brief relationship with a man she met in a bar, JJ became pregnant. Seeking prenatal care in a community health clinic, a compassionate administrative assistant took a personal interested in JJ. She helped her get housing in a program for homeless female Veterans and job coaching. It only takes one person to change the trajectory of another person's life.

So, what is the impact to Main Street if we don't mobilize? Let's assume that any Veteran who has passed the five year mark is in a "safety zone" for becoming newly homeless. So, any post-9/11 Veteran who has separated from the Service since 2009 is still at risk for homelessness. For the sake of argument, let's call that 40% of the 2.2M Veterans already home—880,000 new Veterans. Now, we need to add in the 1M new Veterans we may see over the next four years, creating an at-risk population of 1.88M people. If 4% of these Veterans become homeless, that will add 75,200 Veterans to the newly homeless Veteran population between now and 2021.

And, what is the cost to Main Street? Homeless shelters cost about $8,000 a year per homeless person housed. The average homeless person has longer hospitalizations, at a cost of an extra $2,000 per visit (and, remember, most homeless people do not have health insurance to cover these costs). Many homeless people have substance abuse problems, at a cost of $10,000 or more per person for treatment. Homeless people are more likely to be put in jail, at an average cost of $14,000 per person per year. Add that all up and we are looking at nearly $3B annually in extra expenses to our local governments....much of it avoidable if we help today's military transition well.

And, there are great organizations to help communities address Veteran homelessness, at no cost to the community. The National Coalition for Homeless Veterans can help communities hold a Stand Down, a successful program offered in many states that helps Veterans get into the VA system for benefits and supportive services. The Home Depot Foundation has committed $80M to help communities address Veteran Homelessness through a community grant program. And, a 17% decrease in Veteran homelessness proves that when communities mobilize, it makes a huge difference. Way to go team!

SUBSTANCE ABUSE

Like homelessness, substance abuse in the military is a good news-bad news affair. The most recent Department of Defense study revealed a decrease in smoking and use of illegal drugs. However, there was a significant increase in the misuse of prescription medications, now standing at 11% of all Service Members. Most serious was the increase in alcohol abuse among active duty Service Members: 20% reported heavy drinking and 47 % reported binge drinking at least once. Those who work with Veterans seeking substance abuse treatment find that the vast majority of these Veterans developed their substance abuse problem while on active duty, not after returning home. So, we must assume that coming home will not magically eliminate alcohol and prescription drug abuse and addiction in our military coming home. This will need to be addressed on Main Street.

Gina's friends were surprised when she enlisted in the Guard after college. It gave her a sense of purpose and she enjoyed the camaraderie of drill weekends. Her friends thought it was a hoot to smuggle liquor to her in mouthwash bottles when she deployed. When her boyfriend broke up with her, she began to drink heavily. Her friends, trying to be helpful and believing her story that she didn't have access to adequate care while deployed, were willing to get prescriptions and send them to her.

After she got home and narrowly avoided a drunk driving arrest, Gina realized she had a problem. But, she was afraid to go for help for fear that she would be kicked out of the Guard. Gina eventually told her pastor what was going on and he helped her get confidential help through her church. Gina now attends Alcoholics Anonymous regularly and she reaches out confidentially to other soldiers who she believes have substance abuse problems.

The average cost of substance abuse treatment is about $10,000. That sounds like a lot but now consider the direct costs to community systems for problems associated with ongoing untreated substance abuse: poverty, homelessness, mental health issues, suicide, domestic abuse, child maltreatment, hospitalizations, treatment for HIV and hepatitis, drunk driving arrests, and incarceration. Secondary costs include things like long term financial harm to families, children who arrive in school needing supportive services, foster care, and loss of productivity for people who are victims of drunk driving accidents or violent crimes. I have to confess that I don't have the skills to estimate the direct costs of all of that, but if you remember the $1:$9 rule, I am guessing you can see how a $10,000 substance abuse treatment program could easily save $90,000.

INCARCERATION

It is really hard to find good information on incarcerated Veterans. The most recent data we have dates back to 2004! And, good or bad, right or wrong, fair or unfair, this is a problem that will fall squarely on Main Street.

An August 2012 NBC investigative report from the San Francisco Bay area shows an alarming rise in the number of Veterans in the criminal justice system. San Francisco saw a 58% jump in the number of post-9/11 Veteran arrests over the previous 18 months. In Santa Clara County, the number of Veteran arrests tripled. Anecdotal evidence from law enforcement, judicial systems, and Veteran-serving groups themselves indicate that this is a growing problem.

The dramatic increase in communities establishing self-funded Veteran Courts, a diversion program that focuses on treatment not punishment for Veterans with mental health issues and other transition challenges, strongly suggests that this is a serious problem for Main Street. In the absence of Veterans Courts, the annual cost to incarcerate a single person is roughly $20,000 per year, not including the costs of arrest, adjudication, and re-entry as well as the costs to families of the incarcerated.

However, a February 2013 University of Syracuse study shows that today's Veterans are less than half as likely as other Veterans to be incarcerated. Unless we have accurate information on the scope and nature of Veteran incarceration, we will not be able to effectively address or prevent it. America's colleges and universities could make a significant contribution here. And, it would help if police departments and courts began recording the numbers of military coming through their systems.

And, last but not least, we have domestic abuse and child maltreatment. A DoD report, released in 2012, reported a 30% increase in domestic violence and a 43% increase in child abuse in military families. These are not inherently bad families but young families who are coping with more stress than they can manage and a serious lack of support systems.

> Lindsay and her husband, Mark, a Navy commander, had been married for ten years. They had two children. After Mark's second deployment, he returned home with what appeared to Lindsay to be PTSD. He started to drink heavily. Mark was afraid to go for help for fear that his Marine buddies would think he was weak. He was also afraid that it might prevent his impending promotion.
>
> After a few months home, his verbal and emotional abuse escalated to physical violence with Lindsay and the kids. Lindsay went to talk to the chaplain on base. She didn't want to get Mark in trouble, and she didn't want to end her marriage, but she had been unable to convince him to seek help and she was afraid she would lose her kids if the school found out they were being abused.
>
> Violating confidentiality, the chaplain reported his conversation to Mark's commanding officer. By the end of the day, Mark had been brought before his commanding officer and received a formal reprimand. Because the military takes domestic abuse and child maltreatment seriously, Mark was now at risk for demotion, not being promotable, an "other than honorable" discharge, or even a court martial.

Domestic abuse has far reaching costs and impacts. Immediate costs include doctor and emergency room visits, hospitalizations, domestic abuse hotlines and shelters, counseling, lost wages, police involvement, court involvement, and jail time. Long-term costs include divorce and its subsequent impact on families, failure to thrive in babies and young children, foster care, children arriving in school needing special services, maternal and child depression, secondary PTSD, long-term incarceration, re-entry services, loss of employability, and the list goes on.

With military families falling through the cracks, this is clearly a place where community mental health, schools, religious institutions, and local nonprofits can make a huge difference that lessens human suffering and reduces costs to community budgets.

A NEW SOCIAL CONTRACT FOR AMERICA

A RADICAL CONCEPT FOR SOCIAL CHANGE
THAT BRINGS US BACK TO OUR ROOTS

Huh, a "social contract?"

Allow me a brief review of high school history class. America's founding fathers designed our political system on the idea of a "social contract" where government exists to serve the people. That's the premise of "by the people, for the people." And, the will of the people as a whole ultimately gives power and direction to the government. That's the foundation for democracy and free elections.

Within the collective whole, each individual has a role. Under the social contract, if the State has abused its power, the people have not just the right but the obligation to rise up and take action. That's in a nutshell how we wound up with the Tea Party and the Occupy Movement as well as the heated debates around "class warfare" and income inequality.

FINDING COMMON GROUND

So, what is the status of America's social contract in 2013? Congress is deadlocked. An apparent war is being waged between Congress and the White House. The rich only get richer while the rest of us get poorer. While the inflation-adjusted income for Americans rose a mere 21% between 1979 and 2005, income rose 480% for the richest Americans. Meanwhile, between 2007 and 2010, the wealth of middle class families dropped 39%, eliminating two decades of prosperity.

I'm not advocating for armed revolution on Main Street. But, I am suggesting that perhaps "We the People" need to find common ground, redefine the social contract, stop waiting for a broken system to help us, take back some of our power, and use it to address urgent problems on Main Street. And, in spite of all the issues that divide us, I am suggesting that there is one social issue that we can all agree on....no one in America wants to recreate the long-term outcomes of Vietnam for this generation of Veterans.

If we can all agree on this one principle as common ground, as a place to start, not the endgame, I believe that we can rewrite our social contract so that Main Street and its citizens, civilian and Veteran alike, can

- bridge the military-civilian divide
- prevent the loss of another generation of Veterans
- heal our communities from more than a decade at war
- rediscover the foundation on which we, as citizens on Main Street, can rebuild our communities so that all of America's citizens thrive

Rediscovering America's Greatest Asset: The Power of Community

What if "tradition" is radical? What if the way for America to move ahead is to go back to our collective roots?

What has always made America strong is our ability to overcome challenges and reinvent ourselves, not from the top down but from the bottom up. That is the true power of Main Street and her citizens. Look to the American Revolutionary War, the pioneer movement west, women's suffrage, the civil rights movement....none of these started with the passing of laws or government programs. They started with regular citizens who believed in something and who mobilized the power of community to get the job done.

Unfortunately, during the boom-times of the 1980s and 1990s, communities across America increasingly delegated to government the core services that we traditionally provided as a part of community efforts to look after our own citizens. And, in the process, we forgot how to act like community. In the recent global economic downturn, which many days looks more like a depression than a recession, many of us have felt powerless to help ourselves and our families. And, in our resignation, we lost track of our own power and the inherent leadership each of us holds to make a difference in the world. And, this too shall pass and we shall overcome. We always do. The question is whether we do it the easy way or the hard way.

America has 7.6 million living Vietnam Era Veterans who live by the code, "Never again will one generation of veterans abandon another." Nearly 46 million Boomers, who hold the greatest proportion of individually held wealth in our nation, are increasingly looking for meaningful ways to give back to their communities as they enter retirement. Today's 61 million members of Gen X and adult Millennials are defined by a new spirit of volunteerism and community engagement. More than 8.8 million immigrants eligible for naturalized citizenship are looking to become engaged citizens as they acclimate to Main Street. That's more than 100 million people!

Now imagine if only 1% of us actually step up to the plate and take on self-responsibility to create change in our own communities. Giving just one hour a week, 48 weeks a year, we would generate nearly 50 million volunteer hours every year (no that's not a typo)! Now imagine if we gave two hours a week, or four. Imagine if 2% stepped up, or 4%. The numbers are staggering. And, the scope of change WE can create right in our own communities, without government assistance or outside leadership, has almost no boundaries.

And, if we focus on our post-9/11 Veterans, we not only support them in their transition and proactively work to reduce $1 trillion in long-term care costs, we build a foundation for a new social contract that pays it forward.

How could we do that? That's the topic of the next chapter, "How Can I Help?"

Paying It Forward

Remember how compromise involves giving and taking, that neither side gets everything they want but, ideally, everyone gets what they need....and society is the better for it? Well, social contracts work the same way. So, if the citizens of Main Street step up to support our post-9/11 Veterans, Guard, Reserve, and their families so that they thrive on Main Street, the social contract provides a framework where Veterans, Guard, Reserve, and their families return the favor.

What might that look like, you ask? Simply put, Mr. and Mrs. Post-9/11 Veteran, once you transition back and are settled in, GIVE BACK! Get your spouse or your partner involved. Find ways your kids can help. Donate your time, your professional services, products your company makes, and/or your money. Put your military and leadership skills to work. Be a proactive and engaged community leader. Rally your neighbors to address the critical social issues in your community. And, I must point out that some Veterans are already doing this through organizations like The Mission Continues and Team Rubicon.

Consider the following facts about other groups of people who aren't thriving on Main Street. If this new social contract works, these are the people who were not prioritized while Main Street focuses on helping you, America's Veterans. And, now, they need your help.

- Nearly 16 million children in American, a whopping 22%, live in poverty.
- More than 6 million elderly people live in poverty, a number that has doubled in the past decade and will continue to grow every year.
- More than 37 million Americans, roughly 1 in 8, got emergency food help from one of Main Street's 63,000+ food banks, kitchens, and shelters. This includes more than 14 million children, or 1 in every 5 children in America.
- More than 32 million Americans, or 12% of the population, have severe disabilities, including more than 4 million children.
- As many as 23% of native born Americans cannot read well enough to understand instructions for medications, product information, or a newspaper article.

- At least 35,000 schools across America need renovation at a cost of more than $25 billion.
- About 275,000 prisoners re-enter society each year; sadly, 50% of them are re-incarcerated at a cost of about $30,000 per prisoner per year.

IT'S SIMPLE

So, to boil it down to a few steps, here's the new social contract this book proposes for America....

STEP ONE: Civilians on Main Street step up to support our post-9/11 military so that they transition well because it's the right thing to do and because in the long run it averts a host of serious, costly crises in Hometown America.

STEP TWO: America's post-9/11 military pays it forward by helping to address critical social issues already impacting Hometown America because it's the right thing to do and because in the long run it addresses a host of serious, costly crises on Main Street.

STEP THREE: America's 7.6 million Vietnam era Veterans see how America has learned from our Vietnam experience and they find healing. The 16 million children living in poverty grow up in a culture of self-responsibility and self-empowerment; they pay it forward. America's 46 million Boomers leave the workforce with a sense of purpose and live healthier, more meaningful retirements. The 32 million people with disabilities come to see that they have ability and can contribute to their communities; they pay it forward. America's 8.8 million immigrants eligible for citizenship become citizens and, having found a meaningful place in their communities, pass on a culture of service to their nearly 20 million children, who pay it forward. But, that's a topic for perhaps a sequel to this book, no?

LET'S GET GOING!

THERE ARE AT LEAST 199 WAYS
TO SUPPORT OUR MILITARY COMING HOME

HEY, BUDDY, CAN YOU SPARE 2880 MINUTES?

Remember how just 1% of us giving just one hour a week, 48 weeks a year (or 2880 minutes), would generate nearly 50 million volunteer hours every year? There are at least 199 ways to help....surely one of the ideas below is something you could take on? I'm not asking you to devote your life to supporting our military coming home like I have (but, if you want to volunteer, please shoot me an email at Gretchen@ UntyingTheYellowRibbon.com because team makes a difference). I'm asking you to consider what you can reasonably do in your life, or maybe be a bit unreasonable. Can you do an hour a week? One Saturday afternoon a month? One weekend every four months? One week a year?

Maybe you have your own thing going on. You lost your job and you are job hunting. You are taking care of someone who is sick or disabled. You are getting married, or your child is. You have little kids. You're getting ready to move, or you just moved. Okay, maybe you can't help RIGHT NOW, but could you help, say, in a month or six months? Are you really SO BUSY that you can't find a few hours, even if it's just here and there? If you are care-giving or raising kids, can you involve them in a project? If you are job-hunting, can you find a volunteer gig that you can add to your resume to show that you didn't just sit watching reality TV and eating Cheetos while you waited for the phone to ring?

Whatever you can do, you have a huge THANK YOU from me. And, please keep an eye on my book website (www. UntyingTheYellowRibbon.com) because I intend to have a place where we can share our ideas about how to support our military coming home. And, if you are a city/county manager, or a community leader, or a Veteran transition fanatic, you can check out Troops to Towns (www.TroopsToTowns.org) where you can learn more about our military coming home through community engagement and local government.

The Thing About "Help"

Before we get going here, we need to chat a bit about "helping." No one really likes to admit they need help and we hate to actually ASK for help. But, we all love to have support. As you take on your part to make sure our military thrive back home, consider yourself a supporter not a helper. It sounds picky but it's made a difference in the work I do.

Another thing to ask yourself is, "Am I helping or being of service?" I thank Julio Olalla of the Newfield Network for this subtle distinction. When we "help," our motivation is to make ourselves feel good, regardless of whether our actions are really what the other person needs. Have you ever had someone in a crisis tell you what they really need is quiet time alone....but, you were certain they really didn't mean it so you hovered around, called, emailed, stopped by with muffins? When you bring a family in crisis a meal, do you bring your favorite dish, or theirs? Do you overwhelm them with support? (Guilty as charged on this side of the keyboard, with the best of intentions. Lesson learned.)

What our military coming home need is for us to be of service. Being of service is about making the other person feel good, even if we don't get that "do-gooder boost." It may mean stepping back and waiting to be asked. It may mean discretely helping someone and not getting the pats on the back from your church friends. It may mean doing something you don't like to do because that's really what the other person needs. It may mean rearranging your schedule to accommodate them. Remember, they are the person in transition or crisis.

We are the ones with a bigger emotional bank account to take on something extra. And, when you are truly of service, it feels so good inside to know that you have really, truly been there for the other person that the public kudos or thank you notes actually don't matter.

And, by the by, all of these things work just as well for civilians in transition or crisis. Last I checked, we're all human whether we wear combat boots, pumps, loafers, sneakers, stilettos, slippers....or, my favorite, cowboy boots. Did I mention I moved to Tyler, Texas, America's most Veteran friendly community, just before this book came out? But, that's another story....

Being of Service in Your Neighborhood
Can you....
- Invite a military spouse over for coffee?
- Organize a play date?
- Babysit or have your high schooler be a mother's helper?
- Reach out to military kids, and encourage your kids to?
- Take over carpool duty?
- Help with homework?
- Invite someone to join a civic association committee or the neighborhood watch?
- Show someone around the community?
- Make a community resource list for new military?
- Bake muffins? Bring a meal?
- Do someone's grocery shopping?
- Teach someone to cook?
- Have a barbecue to say hello or good-bye?
- Mow the lawn or shovel snow?
- Plant flowers or a garden?
- Clean or repair gutters?
- Help clear out a garage?
- Repair an appliance?
- Provide plumbing or electrical repair?
- Do laundry? Clean the house?
- Change a light bulb or furnace filter?
- Help pack or unpack?
- Take things to the local shelter?
- Run errands?
- Make phone calls or send emails?
- Write thank you or condolence notes?
- Take a car for repairs or to the car wash?
- Wash a dog or take a pet to the veterinarian?
- Fly a flag and encourage your neighbors to do the same?
    Of course you can!

Being of Service in Your Faith Community
    Can you....
- Look for military among your newcomers?
- Organize a military family welcoming event?
- Have a military appreciation event on Veterans Day?
- Honor the Month of the Military Child in April?
- Have a spa day for military spouses during the Month of the Military Spouse in May?
- Create a local resource list for new members?
- Offer a year of free membership for a new military family?
- Invite people to a bible study group?
- Start a care-giver support group?
- Create a military singles group?
- Talk to your faith leader about getting educated about military, especially moral injury, so they are better prepared to help?
- Have a service that focuses on, and perhaps involves, today's military?
- Organize a military family assistance committee?
- Organize a volunteer day or social event at a local military installation?
- Pack care packages for deployed military?
- Make patriotic themed care kits for local homeless shelters?
- Create self-care packages for the moms at Fisher House?
- Assemble to-do bags for kids at Fisher House?
- Host a cookout for a local Wounded Warrior brigade?
- Organize a church-military softball game?
- Teach kids about their military peers in Sunday school?
- Use the Bible to teach kids about military through history?
- Host an Easter Egg Hunt or Christmas party for military kids?
    Of course you can!

Being of Service in the Public Schools
    Can you....
- Create a welcome program for military families?
- Create a resource list for new families?
- Start a buddy program for new military families?
- Encourage teachers to incorporate age-appropriate military themes into their lessons or to tie lessons to current events?
- Offer to bring in or organize a special activity focusing on today's military?
- Organize an assembly where kids learn patriotic songs or other military/historical topics?
- Organize a special event in April to recognize the Month of the Military Child?
- Volunteer to tutor military kids, especially in Wounded Warrior families?
- Donate books that feature military kids to the school library?
- Bake a special treat for a military holiday?
- Help create a military-themed bulletin board or hallway display?
- Bring your orchestra or chorus to a wounded warrior unit?
- Talk to your principal or other school leadership to make sure that they know about the Interstate Compact?
- Petition you legislators if you are in one of the states that still refuses to participate in the Compact?
- Work with your school administrators to help them come up with a plan to implement the Compact?
- Send cards to deployed military or Wounded Warriors?
- Make Hero Badges for kids living in Fisher House?
- Collect books or toys for kids in Fisher House?
- Organize a care package project?
    Of course you can!

Being of Service in Your Business or Workplace

Can you....

- Donate goods or services?
- Offer military discounts?
- Hold a military appreciation event?
- Help someone write a resume?
- Do mock interviews?
- Provide a free workshop for transitioning military?
- Provide a suit for an interview?
- Get someone business cards or a briefcase?
- Discount your rates?
- Make introductions to local employers?
- Help someone organize informational interviews?
- Mentor a job seeker or new business owner?
- Take someone to a Chamber event or BNI?
- Let someone job shadow you?
- Bring on an intern?
- Provide someone with part-time work?
- Pay your staff for work done to help a local nonprofit?
- Host a fundraiser?
- Let a Veteran-serving nonprofit use your conference room? Make copies?
- Sponsor/host public service announcements on the radio?
- Sponsor/host free print or digital ads?
- Donate business books?
- Learn about TBI, PTSD, and accommodations?
- Sponsor a Veteran event at your Chamber?
- Start a Veterans Committee?
- Hold a local job fair?
- Talk to businesses about hiring Veterans?
- Make your workplace Veteran friendly?
- Hire a Veteran as full-time permanent employee?

Of course you can!

Being of Service in Health and Wellness
    Can you....
- Make sure your social workers and community mental health are trained in PTSD, TBI, and military suicide?
- Donate or discount services?
- Hold a workshop for transitioning military?
- Become a Tricare provider?
- Learn about military transition issues as they pertain to your specialty?
- Encourage your colleagues to get trained in appropriate Veteran-related issues?
- Organize a training event relevant to your field?
- Take the time to ask your patients if they are military?
- Help them get related services if they need them?
- Provide community resource guides?
- Help transitioning military get health insurance?
- Look for signs of abuse in military families? Have the courage to ask questions?
- Work to de-stigmatize mental health services for your patients?
- Have your staff wear flag or yellow ribbon pins?
- Train your staff on Veteran issues?
- Train medical health care providers on the benefits of your modality if you are in the alternative wellness field?
- Learn how to refer to organizations like Give an Hour, Wounded Warrior Project, and Homeward Deployed?
- Offer a community training on PTSD or TBI?
- Do a community training on suicide prevention?
- Volunteer your services at a local shelter, Veteran serving organization, or Fisher House?
- Write an article for your local newspaper or professional journal? Do a radio interview?
    Of course you can!

Being of Service in Law Enforcement and the Judicial System

Can you....

- Track the number of Veterans, Guard, and Reserve coming through your systems so that America can start to assess the rate of Veterans involved in "the system?"
- Create better working relationships with military MPs if you are a military installation community?
- Train your employees in military issues so that they have a military friendly presence?
- Educate judges and lawyers about PTS and TBI as they relate to committing crimes?
- Start a Veterans Court diversion program?
- Have a resource list available for military families who have a primary breadwinner involved in the legal system?
- Expand support services for military families who have a primary breadwinner involved in the legal system?
- Train your police and first responders about responding to suspected PTSD and TBI during a confrontation?
- Create a response plan to "death by cop" incidents?
- Establish a "mental health SWAT Team?"
- Offer job shadowing or internships for Veterans?
- Mentor or hire job seeking Veterans who want to work in law enforcement?
- Work with your state legislators to make licensing and credentialing for EMT positions easier for Veteran combat medics?

Of course you can!

Being of Service in City/County Government

This arena is the focus of Troops to Towns (www.TroopsToTowns.org) but I'm going to give you a teaser.

Can you....

- Put up flags on military-related holidays?
- Have a parade or other community event on Veterans Day, Flag Day, Memorial Day, etc.?
- Organize a community military appreciation event?
- Hold a community covenant?
- Train local government employees in military issues so that they have a military friendly presence?
- Create a community awareness plan to bridge the military-civilian divide?
- Create an open door policy for local Veteran-serving organizations?
- Create a community asset map of Veteran services?
- Initiate dialogue between your Veteran-serving organizations, encouraging them to collaborate?
- Establish a cross-sector Veteran Community Roundtable supported by the mayor, city manager, and town council?
- Contribute staff time to support Veteran efforts?
- Establish job shadowing and internships for Veterans?
- Increase hiring of Veterans in local government?
- Include a line item in your budget for Veterans?
- Become a Community Blueprint community?
- Become a Yellow Ribbon community?
- Apply for a Sea of Goodwill Award or Vet City designation?
- Create a Veteran Strategic Plan?
- Create and fund a Veteran Service office?
- Work with your Chamber(s) and economic development council to create military friendly policies and incentives for Veteran-owned businesses?

Of course you can!

QUESTIONS YOU MAY HAVE ABOUT THIS BOOK

I LOVED IT! HOW CAN I ORDER MORE COPIES?

Okay, you can't blame a girl for hoping you loved it, can you? You can order up to 100 copies of the book in soft-cover, Kindle, or Nook versions at

www.UntyingTheYellowRibbon.com

www.Amazon.com

Bulk copies of the book in soft-cover and licenses for Kindle and Nook versions are available. by contacting us at Sales@UntyingTheYellowRibbon.com. Special pricing is available for cities, counties, school systems, colleges and universities, nonprofits, and associations.

HOW CAN I USE THIS BOOK FOR MY ORGANIZATION'S FUNDRAISING?

The goal of writing this book is to create large scale social change that supports today's military in transition while strengthening Hometown America. We will work with other organizations whose missions align, creating an affiliate relationship where you will keep a portion of the profits of sales of the book to supplement the work you do with Veterans or in your community. Inquiries can be made to Sales@UntyingTheYellowRibbon.com.

WHAT IF I HAVE A COMMENT ON OR TESTIMONIAL FOR THE BOOK?

You can email us at Feedback@UntyingTheYellowRibbon.com with your comments, concerns, suggestions, disagreements, corrections, testimonials, ideas, or any other politely worded feedback. We will make every effort to reply to polite feedback.

Frankly, if a teenage heart-throb can write an autobiography and Hollywood starlets are quoted as experts on humanitarian aid then, tongue in cheek, I offer an unequivocal, "Yes! I have the credentials to write this book."

With a less irreverent tone, I have a graduate degree and a strong research background. I have been working on military transition issues since 2006. Since 2009, I have worked with passion or obsession, depending on who you ask, to reinvent the transition period for our young transitioning military. The focus of that work has been exclusively on the transition phase, with a focus on community-based strategies for prevention.

As a committed lifelong learner, supported by the gifts of intelligence and education, I have taken a deep dive into the research and technical approaches to transition. I have spent the past seven years building an organization and programs to address these issues with evidence-based approaches combined in innovative ways that reflect my curvilinear life path. Homeward Deployed's coaching programs, which I designed, have been positively reviewed by an increasingly long list of high profile people within the military/Veteran arena as well as within the coaching world. Our coaching and community mobilization programs have been well received by post-9/11 Veterans, Guard, and Reserve themselves as well as community leaders. I could do some name dropping but it's not my style.

In the interest of full disclosure, I am not myself a Veteran, Guard, Reservist, military spouse, wounded warrior care-giver, or family member of someone killed in action. While my dad served for four years as an Army physician during the Vietnam War and we lived in Okinawa, I do not consider myself an Army brat. I am at heart a civilian chick from Main Street who in 2006 became deeply concerned by what I saw, and continue to see, happening with our young military and their families. Because I do not come from within the system, I bring a different perspective to military transition issues. My intention is to use my unique perspectives to inspire new conversations that lead to exploring non-traditional pathways to effective solutions that help our young military in transition thrive.

Ultimately, you will decide whether I have the credentials to write this book, based on whether you have taken away something of value after reading it.

WHY IS THE FOCUS POST-9/11 VETERANS?

Truthfully, I have been accused of "not caring" about older generations of Veterans. Let's be clear, my dad is a Vietnam-era Veteran who served for four years as a physician. When I look back on how I grew up, I see the fingerprint of my dad's military experience on my family life. I am not insensitive to the factors that have and continue to impact these Veterans. However, the vast majority of our Vietnam Veterans grew into productive citizens and many have already comfortably entered their retirement years. As the Boomer Generation, they hold the largest share of individual wealth of any generation of Veterans. As for those who have not transitioned well, meant with all love and genuine respect, after 40 years these Veterans are realistically not likely to transition now or in the future. For these Veterans, we need to provide compassionate care, the same compassionate care that we should provide all Americans who for whatever reason cannot care for themselves.

And, what about the Gulf War Veterans? The Gulf War lasted seven months and involved 700,000 American Service Members with 294 killed. Roughly 250,000 Service Members, or 36%, have been treated for "Gulf War Syndrome." The impact on the families of the fallen, as well as those still managing the after-effects of Gulf War Syndrome, is significant. However, America has not seen the serious transition issues or sky-rocketing long-term care costs that we see with our post-9/11 Veterans.

If you read the chapter on the military-civilian divide, you know that my focus is on preventing losing another generation of Veterans. I believe we still have a window of opportunity to support our post-9/11 Veterans, Guard, Reserve, and their families onto pathways of permanent economic stability and family resilience. If we muster our resources and do prevention well, we can address the long-term care and human costs for this generation of Veterans. The time for prevention for our Vietnam and Gulf War Veterans, regrettably, has passed.

WHY ARE STATISTICS FOOTNOTED?

This book is intended to give real people who live on Main Street, from America's proverbial "Joe the Plumber" to the mayor, a solid understanding of what is happening with our post-9/11 Veterans. It is absolutely not the case that I think Joe or his mayor can't read statistics. I believe that what is useful is a short, concise, easy to read little book that gives busy, information overloaded Americans a basic understanding of today's Veterans.... something in-between Reader's Digest and Scientific American.

For those of you who come from academia or the land of policy wonks, I am a fellow research nerd with some letters after my name and a list of publications on my resume. So, for you, I have included sources for my numbers and statistics. Yes, I do understand that often the numbers are not the numbers and there are serious turf wars about whose numbers to use. Please keep in mind that this little book is intentionally not written as a research publication or dissertation. It is not focused on changing national policy although, truthfully, I have hopes it might change how we think about and address the issues of post-9/11 Veteran transition.

MISSION: To provide leaders on Main Street with free and low-cost solutions to meet the transition needs of today's military and their families coming home

KEY NEED ADDRESSED: Local governments and community leaders need a central hub focusing on the unique needs of those providing community-based support to transitioning military and their families on Main Street. Troops to Towns provides a robust set of tools, trainings, and resources for those responsible for supporting our military coming back to Hometown America.

Service Areas and Key Outcomes

- Leadership Pipeline: Strengthen the leadership pipeline in city/county management by integrating today's transitioning military.
- Education: Educate community leaders through a single organization about resources, best practices, emerging trends, and innovative solutions to meet the transition needs of America's 3M+ post-9/11 military, focusing specifically on the unmet needs on Main Street.
- Implementation: Support community leaders through successful implementation to bring these resources and programs to their Hometown.
- Sustainability: Establish a learning community to focus on sustainable Veteran transition on Main Street for future generations of military using a 360° ecological model.
- Citizen Engagement: Rekindle the spirit of community engagement through shared purpose in a way that rebuilds civic participation and leadership.

Expected Launch Date: Summer 2013

MISSION: Supporting the successful transition of our post-9/11 Veterans, Guard, & Reserve so that they thrive on Main Street, strengthening military families and Hometown America

KEY NEED ADDRESSED: Roughly 70% of Service Members report serious challenges in returning to civilian life. Support for military families, wounded warrior care-givers, and the families of the fallen is often non-existent back home on Main Street.

Core Programs

TRANSITION BOOT CAMP PORTFOLIO: Putting Veterans, Guard, and Reserve to work in small businesses on Main Street America, where they actually live and where 100% of net new jobs are actually created, including entrepreneurship (self-employment) as an important pathway to economic resilience.

- Transition Coaching
- Employment Coaching
- Entrepreneurship/Business Coaching
- Coaching-on-Campus
- Wounded-Warrior Employer Coaching

FAMILY RESILIENCE PORTFOLIO: Empowering Military and Veteran families to maintain strong family bonds while moving through the cycles of deployment and successfully reintegrating as a strong, resilient family team, honoring the losses and changes that come with deployment, return from duty, and separation from the Service.

- Family Coaching, including Active Duty LGBT
- Wounded Warrior Care-giver Coaching
- Employment Coaching for Spouses of the Fallen
- Coaching-on-Campus for Children/Siblings of the Fallen

Gretchen's Recommended Reading and Viewing

The Day After He Left for Iraq
By Melissa Seligman

Homeland Season 2 (television series)
Starring Claire Danes and Damian Lewis

The Hurt Locker (movie)
Starring Jeremy Renner

In an Instant: A Family's Journey of Love and Healing
By Lee Woodruff

Individual and Community Responses to Disaster and Trauma
Edited by Ursano, McCaughey, Fullerton, and Raphael

In Search of the Warrior Spirit
By Richard Strozzi-Heckler

A Mindful Nation
By Congressman Tim Ryan

Rule Number Two: Lessons I Learned in a Combat Hospital
By Heidi Kraft

Soul Repair: Recovering from Moral Injury After War
By Rita Nakashimi Brock and Gabriella Latini

The Invisible War (documentary)
Starring Helen Benedict and Kori Cioka

Moment of Truth in Iraq
By Michael Yon

Restrepo (documentary)

Shadow of the Sword
By Jeremiah Workman

Taking Chance (movie)
Starring Kevin Bacon

The Things They Carried
By Tim O'Brien

The Three Trillion Dollar War: The True Cost of the Iraq Conflict
By Linda Bilmes and Joseph Stiglitz

The War Tapes (documentary)
Starring Zack Bazzi

The Warriors Heart: Becoming a Man of Compassion and Courage
By Eric Greitens

The Way of Transition: Embracing Life's Most Difficult Moments
By William Bridges

The Way We Get By (documentary)

Why People Die by Suicide
By Thomas Joiner

The Will to Resist: Soldiers Who Refuse to Fight in Iraq and Afghanistan
By Dahr Jamail and Chris Hedges

Yellow Birds
By Kevin Powers

Great Organizations to Know (and Use)

Army Community Covenant
www.army.mil/community

Community Blueprint
www.pointsoflight.org/programs/military-initiatives/community-blueprint

Fisher House
www.FisherHouse.org

Give an Hour
www.GiveAnHour.org

Iraq and Afghanistan Veterans of America
www.IAVA.org

National Coalition for Homeless Veterans
www.NCHV.org

National Military Families Association
www.MilitaryFamily.org

Operation Gratitude
www.OpGratitude.org

Operation Homefront
www.OperationHomefront.net

Operation Second Chance
www.OperationSecondChance.org

Our Military Kids
www.OurMilitaryKids.org

Salute America's Heroes
www.saluteheroes.org

Soldiers' Angels
www.SoldiersAngels.org

Student Veterans of America
www.StudentVeterans.org

Swords to Plowshares
www.Swords-to-Plowshares.org

Team Rubicon
www.TeamRubiconUSA.org

The Mission Continues
www.MissionContinues.org

Tragedy Assistance Program for Survivors
www.TAPS.org

United Service Organization (USO)
www.USO.org

Warrior Gateway
www.WarriorGateway.org

Wounded Warrior Project
www.WoundedWarriorProject.org

REFERENCES

THE MILITARY CIVILIAN DIVIDE: PART ONE

Number of post-9/11 Veterans (2.2M)
http://iava.org/success-story/iava-vets-get-ahead-streetwise-partners

Number in the National Guard and Reserve (850,000+)
DOD report Demographics 2010

Number of Gulf War Era Veterans (2.6 M = 4.8M – 2.2M)
http://www.census.gov/newsroom/releases/archives/facts_for_features_special_
editions/cb11-ff23.html

Number of Vietnam Era Veterans(7.6M)
http://www.census.gov/newsroom/releases/archives/facts_for_features_special_
editions/cb11-ff23.html

Demographics of Active Duty Military (67% under 30)
http://www.slideshare.net/pastinson/us-military-active-duty-demographic-pro-
file-presentation

Post-9/11 Veteran perception of the transition process
All Volunteer Force: From Military to Civilian Service by Mary McNaught Yonk-
man and John Marshall Bridgeland (Civic Enterprise)

Physical Injuries
http://www.newsu.org/course_files/SRIpdfResources/VeteransIssues.pdf

Traumatic Brain Injury (TBI)
http://www.swords-to-plowshares.org/wp-content/uploads/IVP-Refer-
ence-Guide-10.11-1.pdf?9d7bd4

Unemployment

http://www.armytimes.com/news/2012/02/military-young--vets-unemployment-could-reach-50-percent-020212w/

Homelessness

http://battleland.blogs.time.com/2012/05/08/battered-and-bruised-minds-lead-to-homelessness/

Post-Traumatic Stress Disorder

http://www.navytimes.com/news/2012/03/military-times-2012-poll-ptsd-diagnosis-rates-rise-female-troops-031212w/

Emotional Trauma

http://pewresearch.org/databank/dailynumber/?NumberID=1456

Suicide

http://www.nytimes.com/2012/06/09/us/suicides-eclipse-war-deaths-for-us-troops.html/

Mental Health Issues

http://www.swords-to-plowshares.org/wp-content/uploads/IVP-Reference-Guide-10.11-1.pdf?9d7bd4

Substance Abuse

http://www.newsu.org/course_files/SRIpdfResources/VeteransIssues.pdf

http://www.swords-to-plowshares.org/wp-content/uploads/IVP-Reference-Guide-10.11-1.pdf?9d7bd4

Military Sexual Trauma

http://bhpr.hrsa.gov/grants/areahealtheducationcenters/ta/Trainings/materials/ta209substanceabuse.pdf

Student Veterans

http://usnews.nbcnews.com/_news/2012/07/02/12509343-thousands-of-veterans-failing-in-latest-battlefield-college?lite

Domestic Abuse and Child Maltreatment

http://www.foxnews.com/us/2012/01/19/army-reports-suicides-down-but-violent-crimes-up/

Violent Crime

http://www.foxnews.com/us/2012/01/19/army-reports-suicides-down-but-violent-crimes-up/

The Cost of Care

The New York Times July 28, 2011

http://seattletimes.nwsource.com/html/nationworld/2016936178_usiraqcosts05.html

http://threetrilliondollarwar.org/

THE MILITARY CIVILIAN DIVIDE: PART TWO

Cost of the War
The Three Trillion Dollar War by Joseph Stiglitz and Linda Bilmes
www.ThreeTrillionDollarWar.org

Bring the War Dollars Home
http://articles.cnn.com/2011-06-20/us/mayors.conference_1_mayors-paul-soglin-war-resolution?_s=PM:US

Cost of DeWitt Hospital
http://en.wikipedia.org/wiki/Fort_Belvoir_Community_Hospital

Cost of Army Uniforms

http://www.businessinsider.com/the-army-admits-it-made-a-big-5-billion-mis-take-choosing-its-uniforms-2012-6

Civilian Unemployment

http://www.tradingeconomics.com/united-states/unemployment-rate

Veteran Unemployment

http://www.armytimes.com/news/2012/07/military-veterans-young-unemploy-ment-rate-big-drop-070612w/

Wages

http://www.deptofnumbers.com/income/us/

http://usatoday30.usatoday.com/money/economy/income/2006-02-23-fed-in-comes_x.htm

http://www.washingtonpost.com/opinions/how-can-we-save-money-on-troops-pay-and-benefits-lets-ask-the-troops/2013/04/19/8f9f0258-a5d8-11e2-b029-8fb7e977ef71_story.html?hpid=z5

Number Without Health Insurance

http://www.c-spanvideo.org/program/305056-5

Cost of Post-9/11 GI Bill Benefits

http://www.nctimes.com/news/opinion/perspective/vets-who-won-gi-bill-now-lobby-to-reign-in/article_1b19eba7-1c5c-5e62-89f6-ea9d73d136a2.html

Student Loan Debt

http://www.reuters.com/article/2011/11/03/us-usa-student-loans-idUSTRE7A-24HI20111103

Background Vietnam War Information
http://en.wikipedia.org/wiki/Vietnam_War

Statistics for Vietnam, Gulf War, OIF, OEF
http://www1.va.gov/opa/publications/factsheets/fs_americas_wars.pdf

OIF/OEF Statistics
http://siadapp.dmdc.osd.mil/personnel/CASUALTY/gwot_component.pdf

Traumatic Brain Injuries for Post-9/11 Veterans
http://www.ptsd.va.gov/professional/newsletters/research-quarterly/v21n1.pdf
http://www.rand.org/multi/military/veterans.html

PTSD
http://www.military.com/veterans-report/va-says-ptsd-affects-most-oif-oef-vets?ESRC=vr.nl

Background Gulf War Information
http://en.wikipedia.org/wiki/Gulf_War

The VA
http://www.va.gov/about_va/mission.asp
http://www.va.gov/about_va/vahistory.asp

Backlog of Cases
http://www.vawatchdog.org/The_Backlog.html
http://www.cbsnews.com/8301-18563_162-57469804/massive-veterans-af-fairs-backlog-leaves-half-a-million-waiting-for-benefits/

VA Usage by Veterans
http://www.veteranshealth.org/about.html

Rape at VA Hospitals

http://www.marinecorpstimes.com/news/2011/06/military-VA-sexual-assaults-report-response-060811w/

Transition GPS

http://www.davmembersportal.org/national/Shared%20Documents/TAPS_Improve.pdf

Hiring Our Heroes Job Fairs

http://www.franchisetimes.com/content/story.php?article=02392

Small Businesses and Jobs

http://web.sba.gov/faqs/faqIndexAll.cfm?areaid=24

http://www.businessweek.com/articles/2012-04-26/small-business-job-creation-is-stronger-than-we-think

http://www.politifact.com/virginia/statements/2011/dec/30/eric-cantor/cantor-says-small-businesses-create-70-percent-us-/

Tax Credits

http://www.doleta.gov/business/incentives/opptax/PDF/veterans_fact_sheet12_1_2011.pdf

http://www.doleta.gov/business/incentives/opptax/PDF/employers_wotc_veterans_brochure_5_24_12.pdf

Who Are America's Post-9/11 Military?

The demographic data for Active Duty, Guard, and Reserve comes from a DOD report Demographics 2010.

The anecdotes and personal stories come from six years of work with transitioning military. Names and identifying characteristics have been changed to maintain confidentiality with the exception of quoted stories.

http://www.militaryhomefront.dod.mil/12038/Project%20Documents/Military-HOMEFRONT/Reports/2010_Demographics_Report.pdf

Panetta Quote
http://www.defense.gov/news/newsarticle.aspx?id=117454

USERRA Law
http://www.dol.gov/compliance/guide/userra.htm
http://veterans.house.gov/witness-testimony/mr-theodore-ted-l-daywalt

Don't Ask, Don't Tell Background
http://en.wikipedia.org/wiki/Don't_ask,_don't_tell

Divorce Rates
http://www.usatoday.com/news/military/story/2011-12-13/military-divorce-rate-increases/51888872/1
http://www.huffingtonpost.com/2011/04/12/divorce-rate-for-women-in-military_n_848125.html

Domestic Abuse
http://www.foxnews.com/us/2012/01/19/army-reports-suicides-down-but-violent-crimes-up/

Military Children
www.AmericasPromise.org

Veteran Numbers come from Drew Helmer's presentation
http://www.warrelatedillness.va.gov/WARRELATEDILLNESS/education/conferences/2011-aug/conferences-slides-aug-2011.asp

Student Veterans
http://usnews.nbcnews.com/_news/2012/07/02/12509343-thousands-of-veterans-failing-in-latest-battlefield-college?lite

Vietnam Veterans Memorial

http://en.wikipedia.org/wiki/Vietnam_Veterans_Memorial

Wounded Warriors

http://www.newsu.org/course_files/SRIpdfResources/VeteransIssues.pdf

http://www.swords-to-plowshares.org/wp-content/uploads/IVP-Reference-Guide-10.11-1.pdf?9d7bd4

http://www.nytimes.com/2011/06/02/health/02brain.html

Operation Impact

http://careers.northropgrumman.com/operation_impact.html

http://www.northropgrumman.com/about_us/faq/index.html#rev

Care-giver Act of 2012

http://www.gpo.gov/fdsys/pkg/PLAW-111publ163/pdf/PLAW-111publ163.pdf

Contractors

http://costsofwar.org/sites/default/files/articles/11/attachments/Lutz%20US%20and%20Coalition%20Casualties.pdf

WHEN BAD THINGS HAPPEN TO GOOD VETERANS

Much of the information here, with the exception of the citations below, comes from a Behavioral Health Certification, "Serving Our Veterans," I completed in December 2012. The Certificate was piloted by We Are Virginia Veterans. It was co-designed by The National Council for Community Behavioral Healthcare, the Center for Deployment Psychology, and Essential Learning LLC.

TBI

http://www.tbicommunty.org

http://www.nytimes.com/2011/06/02/health/02brain.html?_r=0

PTSD

http://www.fas.org/sgp/crs/misc/R41921.pdf

http://news.harvard.edu/gazette/story/2012/05/signs-of-progress-against-ptsd/

http://nation.time.com/2012/02/23/they-dont-seem-to-get-better/

The National Center for PTSD/ Deparment of Veterans Affairs

www.ptsd.va.gov

Polytrauma

The National Center for PTSD/ Deparment of Veterans Affairs: www.ptsd.va.gov

Secondary PTSD

http://spousebuzz.com/blog/2011/06/is-secondary-ptsd-overdiagnosed.html

Moral Injury

http://www.ptsd.va.gov/professional/newsletters/research-quarterly/v23n1.pdf

http://video.foxnews.com/v/2245605536001/iraq-war-chaplain-on-faiths-role-in-helping-soldiers-/

MST

http://www.vanityfair.com/online/oscars/2013/02/invisible-war-oscar-nominated-documentary

http://www.thedailybeast.com/articles/2011/12/13/judge-dismisses-epidemic-of-rape-in-military-case.html

http://www.nytimes.com/2013/03/13/opinion/sexual-assaults-and-military-justice.html?_r=0

http://nation.time.com/2012/06/20/a-different-kind-of-invisible-wound/

http://www.newsy.com/videos/report-slams-va-sexual-assault-rape-responses/

http://www.nydailynews.com/news/world/25-increase-sex-assault-combat-zones-wait-sober-pentagon-watchdog-article-1.368800

Suicide

http://www.huffingtonpost.com/joseph-bobrow/veteran-suicide-rate_b_2936244.html

http://www.huffingtonpost.com/joseph-bobrow/veteran-suicide-60-minutes_b_2849668.html

http://www.forbes.com/sites/timworstall/2013/02/02/but-there-isnt-an-epidemic-of-suicide-in-the-us-military/

http://www.forbes.com/sites/melaniehaiken/2013/02/05/22-the-number-of-veterans-who-now-commit-suicide-every-day/

http://usnews.nbcnews.com/_news/2013/01/16/16540098-like-an-airborne-disease-concern-grows-about-military-suicides-spreading-within-families?lite

http://www.cdc.gov/violenceprevention/suicide/consequences.html

Homelessness

http://nation.time.com/2012/05/08/battered-and-bruised-minds-lead-to-homelessness/

http://www.endhomelessness.org/pages/veterans

http://www.endhomelessness.org/pages/cost_of_homelessness

Substance Abuse

http://www.amednews.com/article/20120928/health/309289992/8/

http://www.drugabuse.gov/publications/topics-in-brief/substance-abuse-among-military-veterans-their-families

http://www.drugfree.org/join-together/alcohol/u-s-military-studying-ways-to-reduce-substance-abuse-among-service-members

http://www.phoenixhouse.org/news-and-views/our-perspectives/for-many-veterans-substance-abuse-begins-overseas/

http://www.endhomelessness.org/pages/cost_of_homelessness

Incarceration

http://www.nbcbayarea.com/investigations/Veterans-Behind-Bars-166063656.html

http://www.justicepolicy.org/news/2861

http://vets.syr.edu/wp-content/uploads/2013/02/ResearchBrief_Tsai2013.pdf

http://www.endhomelessness.org/pages/cost_of_homelessness

Domestic Abuse and Child Maltreatment

http://www.foxnews.com/us/2012/01/19/army-reports-suicides-down-but-violent-crimes-up/

A NEW SOCIAL CONTRACT

Income Disparity

http://www.nytimes.com/2011/09/23/opinion/krugman-the-social-contract.html?_r=1

Wealth Drops 40%

http://www.washingtonpost.com/business/economy/fed-americans-wealth-dropped-40-percent/2012/06/11/gJQAllsCVV_story.html

U.S. Demographics Across Generations

http://en.wikipedia.org/wiki/Demographics_of_the_United_States#Vital_statisticsChildren in Poverty

http://datacenter.kidscount.org/data/acrossstates/Rankings.aspx-?loct=6&by=a&order=a&ind=43&dtm=322&tf=38&gclid=CJbT1oibx7ECFYVg-TAodA2IAtw

Children in Single Parent Homes

http://datacenter.kidscount.org/data/acrossstates/Rankings.aspx-?loct=2&by=a&order=a&ind=107&dtm=432&ch=a&tf=133

Cost of Renovating America's Schools

http://www.rebuildamericasschools.org/

Elderly Poor

http://www.huffingtonpost.com/2012/03/02/senior-citizens-living-expenses_n_1316197.html

http://www.huffingtonpost.com/2011/11/07/supplemental-poverty-measure_n_1080160.html

People with Disabilities

http://www.census.gov/newsroom/releases/archives/facts_for_features_special_editions/cb06-ff10-2.html

Literacy

http://en.wikipedia.org/wiki/Literacy_in_the_United_States

Prisions

http://en.wikipedia.org/wiki/Incarceration_in_the_United_States

Food Banks

http://www.usatoday.com/news/sharing/2010-02-01-hunger_N.htm

http://www.serve.gov/toolkits/food-bank/index.asp

QUESTIONS YOU MAY HAVE ABOUT THIS BOOK

Gulf War

http://en.wikipedia.org/wiki/Gulf_War

Number of Troops in Gulf War

http://www.nationmaster.com/graph/mil_gul_war_coa_for-military-gulf-war-co-alition-forces

Gulf War Syndrome

http://en.wikipedia.org/wiki/Gulf_War_syndrome

www.ingramcontent.com/pod-product-compliance
Lightning Source LLC
Chambersburg PA
CBHW030018290326
41934CB00005B/388